# MORTGAGES AND FORECLOSURE

# MORTGAGES AND FORECLOSURE
## Know your rights

David M. Goldenberg, B.A., LL.B. (Hon.)

**Self-Counsel Press**
*(a division of)*
International Self-Counsel Press Ltd.
Vancouver
Toronto   Seattle

Printed in Canada

First edition: April, 1983
Second edition: October, 1983
Third edition: July, 1985
Fourth edition: February, 1987
Fifth edition: April, 1989


Canadian Cataloguing in Publication Data

Goldenberg, David M.
    Mortgages and foreclosures

    (Self-counsel legal series)
    ISBN 0-88908-853-5

    1. Mortgages — Canada — Popular works.   2. Fore-
closure — Canada — Popular works.   I. Title.   II. Series.
KE752.Z82G66   1989   346.7104'364   C89-091094-4

**Self-Counsel Press**
(a division of)
International Self-Counsel Press Ltd.
1481 Charlotte Road
North Vancouver, British Columbia V7J 1H1

# CONTENTS

# NOTICE TO READERS

# PREFACE

Mortgages - foreclosure - equity - judicial sale: these are words we toss around every day. Some are used as catch words or slang without our really knowing what they mean; some strike fear in our hearts.

Mortgages have been part of our lives for a long time. There is no reason to suspect that they won't continue to play a major role in all our lives. As long as people have the hope and desire to own their own homes, we will need mortgages.

A number of books have been written about mortgages. Most of them are written in "legalese" and are textbooks on mortgages that only lawyers can understand. Worse yet, they invariably emphasize matters from the lender's point of view.

What about your rights as a borrower? How do you apply for a mortgage? What are your ongoing obligations? What can you do if you don't or can't make your payments?

The answers to these questions are usually never supplied in those books. Sometimes the answers involve legal considerations, but most of the time they involve practical or common-sense considerations.

This book is meant to fill the void. It is designed to specifically focus on the borrower's rights, remedies, and obligations with regard to mortgages. It starts with a discussion of what mortgages are and how they work.

It then describes ways in which you apply for or assume a mortgage and what you must do to maintain your mortgage in good standing throughout its term.

Finally, it examines in detail what happens in the unfortunate situation where you simply cannot make your payments. Default under a mortgage is a serious matter and one that can have severe repercussions on every aspect of your life. Therefore, we will spend some time looking at what the lender can do if a default occurs, what you can do, and what legal and non-legal factors you have to consider in dealing with this problem.

# 1

# WHAT IS A MORTGAGE?

## a. HISTORY AND DEVELOPMENT OF MORTGAGES

Even hundreds of years ago, in feudal England, loans were made from a creditor to a debtor using the debtor's land as security. However, these loans were complicated by the fact that the churches in the Middle Ages condemned the lending of money in exchange for interest as the sin of usury. Therefore, it was necessary for lenders to actually take physical possession of the debtor's land when they made a loan in order to avoid the sanction of the church. This became known as a "live gage" (meaning pledge). If the debtor failed to repay the money, the lender was entitled to retain the land until the loan was paid. If the borrower did not repay the debt, the land became the lender's land permanently.

Although this method of lending money circumvented the strict rules of the church, it became cumbersome for the lender. There were many situations where the lender was unwilling or unable to take actual physical possession of the land in order to make the loan. Naturally, debtors were not thrilled either with the idea of giving up possession of their land; in most cases they needed the loan to make some improvements on the land. The loan, therefore, was self-defeating.

As the commercial world became more sophisticated, the laws were adapted to allow the lender to make the loan without taking possession of the land. This developed into the "mort" (dead or passive) gage. Although the terms of the loan were extremely strict, the debtor was entitled to retain possession of the land. The lender had the right to take over the land if payments were not made, but the borrower could stay in possession at least until the due date of the loan.

As this area of the law developed, the courts of the "common law" regulated mortgages. The common law came out of a system of reporting individual decisions on a case by case basis and using the precedents obtained from those decisions to apply to future cases. However, this strict reliance on earlier decisions lead to an inflexible system where the fairness or justice of particular situations were not taken into consideration.

Because of the harshness of the common law, individuals began to petition the king for relief. The king had the right to override the decisions of the common law courts.

In certain situations, the king changed the law to add a measure of fairness or justice to a particular decision. This work was soon transferred to the king's advisors, known as the king's chancellors, and over the years a separate body of law known as the courts of equity developed.

It was the courts of equity that granted relief to the borrower when the courts of common law would not. Unlike the common law courts, the courts of equity exercised a discretion based on an examination of the individual circumstances in each case.

These two courts, the common law courts and the courts of equity were eventually merged so that today, judges have the ability to operate as judges of both the common law courts and the courts of equity. This means that although the courts can rely on the laws and general principles developed from previous cases, they are also entitled to exercise a judicial discretion and provide equitable remedies in particular circumstances. This is vital in the area of mortgages. Over the centuries the law has recognized the need to regulate loans that involve land as security, especially when that land is a personal residence or a homestead or farmland from which a livelihood is earned.

In dealing with modern situations involving a mortgage, the courts have a vast body of law to refer to. Not only are there myriads of cases that have produced legal principles for the past hundreds of years, but there are also statutes and complex rules of practice in effect that govern the rights of all parties.

But remember, the judges who make the decisions are human beings who also have mortgages, who also are subject to the ups and downs of the economy, and who also are affected by problems of high interest rates and inflation.

Although there is never any express recognition by the courts of those "non-legal elements" of a mortgage problem, they are in fact very important and very relevant. If you wind up in court with mortgage problems, the proper presentation of the case may in fact be the determining factor when the court comes to something like setting a redemption period.

## b. THE LEGAL NATURE OF A MORTGAGE

In all cases a mortgage has two key ingredients. First, the mortgage is a contract between one party who wants to lend money and one party who wants to borrow money. The lender of the money is known as the mortgagee, the borrower is known as the mortgagor. I will use the terms "mortgagee" and "mortgagor" occasionally in this book.

Second, the loan in some way involves the pledge of something owned by the borrower as security for the loan. The lender, in negotiating with the borrower, agrees to lend money to the borrower in return for the repayment of that loan plus some interest. However, the lender, having assessed the risks involved in making the loan and in particular the possibility that the loan might not be repaid, decides that something else is required besides the mortgagor's simple promise to pay. This something extra is normally the pledge of the borrower's land as security. This means that the borrower promises to repay the money plus interest in accordance with the terms of the contract.

If the money is not repaid, the lender has recourse not only against the borrower personally but against the borrower's land. In fact the borrower has placed the lender, with regard to the land that is pledged, in a "secured"

3

position ahead of all other people owed money by the borrower. This is the key point. The borrower may owe money to a number of individuals or companies. The risk to a lender is that if the borrower defaults, the lender would be in the same position as all other creditors of the debtor. However, by having the land as security, the lender is assured of first rights to that land. If a default occurs, all of the other creditors of the debtor rank behind the lender.

Content with the knowledge that he or she will be in a priority position over all other creditors or future creditors, the lender will then make the loan.

The classic definition of a mortgage incorporates these two key elements:

A mortgage is a conveyance of land as a security for the payment of the debt or the discharge of some other obligation for which it is given, the security being redeemable on the payment or discharge of such debt or obligation.

You should also understand exactly what is meant by "land" in this context. By law, land includes not only the raw land that forms part of your property, but also includes everything above the land that is attached and everything below the land. Therefore, all buildings that are built on the land become part of the land and, consequently, become part of the mortgage security. In fact, the building is often worth more than the raw land.

Lenders of residential mortgages examine building values very closely because the value of the house and other buildings on the land go a long way in determining the total value of the "land" and whether or not a loan will be approved.

Because mortgages fall into the category of property and civil rights, the regulation of mortgages is a provincial matter, although some aspects of interest and interest rates are governed federally. Therefore, the laws dealing with mortgages differ from province to province. However, the definition above is valid in all circumstances and for all types of mortgages. Basically only the types of mortgages and mortgage registration and enforcement laws vary.

4

It is not my intention to discuss in detail the various types of contracts involved in loans of this type. Suffice to say that, as in all contracts, the rights, liabilities, and obligations of the parties are stated in the contractual document. Because this is a contract that deals with land, the contract itself must be in writing. Therefore, in many cases, mortgages are written agreements signed by the borrower.

The problem is that most of the mortgage documents you are faced with are long involved agreements with many clauses and full of fine print and legal terms that are incomprehensible not only to most laypeople but to most lawyers as well. Each clause has a meaning and has been ruled on by the courts on many occasions. However, this does not help you, as the borrower, when it comes time to sign the documents. In many cases, people sign a mortgage without thoroughly reviewing the content.

## 1. Legal mortgages

A "legal mortgage" is a mortgage properly registered under the laws of a province. For our purposes, it is not necessary to examine the technicalities involved in this registration process. This information is readily available from the land registry or land title offices in your province. The important point is that to give the lender security and protection prior to and subsequent to making the loan, the mortgage must be properly registered in accordance with the rules and procedures in your province.

The registration systems in each province are designed to allow members of the public to examine titles to property to determine exactly what interests are registered against particular parcels of land. This process is known as searching title. By searching title, anybody can quickly determine whether certain land is subject to any mortgage security interests and can obtain the details of such security.

## 2. Common law mortgages

The key point about common law mortgages is that the legal title to the land is "vested" or transferred into the name of the lender while the loan is outstanding. However, the borrower retains "the equity of redemption." This means that the title to the land is transferred to the lender conditional only upon the borrower repaying the loan. If the borrower does repay the loan, the lender is required by law to return the title to the land to the borrower.

The borrower is entitled to exclusive possession of the land during the time the mortgage is in force and, conversely, the lender is restricted from being on the land. In fact, unless the borrower has in some way breached the terms of the mortgage contract, it would be at the very least a civil offence and perhaps even a criminal offence if the lender attempted to go onto the property.

### 3. Equitable mortgages

Equitable mortgages have also been recognized by the courts. In all provinces, an equitable mortgage is one where the title to the property remains with the borrower.

In many situations, an equitable mortgage can be created simply by giving the lender the title deeds as security. In other words, instead of an actual conveyance of the legal title, the borrower, to symbolize the pledge of security, delivers the actual title papers to the lender, who is entitled to keep those papers until the loan is repaid. Without those title deeds, the borrower cannot sell or further encumber the property.

This type of mortgage has been recognized as being a valid charge in all jurisdictions, although problems can arise when a third party or another lender becomes involved in the situation.

In addition, equitable mortgages in all provinces, except Quebec, can be registered on the title by way of caveat. A caveat is simply a registered notice to the world that there is some form of encumbrance claimed by a lender on the title. This form of encumbrance is often the quickest, simplest and cheapest way of protecting a lender.

An equitable mortgage does create a mortgage contract and with it the obligations and liabilities of the borrower to the lender. In fact, the enforcement procedures for an equitable mortgage are basically the same as the enforcement procedures for both the common law mortgage and the legal mortgage.

## 4. Second and third mortgages

A second and even a third mortgage can be taken out on property already mortgaged. A second mortgage really means a mortgage that is second "in time" or "in priority" to an existing first mortgage.

As discussed earlier, once a first mortgage is registered against a particular property, the lender obtains a priority to the equity in that property ahead of everybody else claiming an interest in it including the owner.

In simple terms, whoever sits on top of the totem pole has first priority to the money received from a sale of the property. If you have no mortgage, then you sit at the top of the totem pole and are entitled to all the money.

However, once you place a first mortgage on your house, your lender takes over top position and you move down a notch to second place. If your house is sold, the lender is entitled to first dibs on all of the sale proceeds required to pay it off in full. The remaining money then goes to you as the owner.

If your property carries a second mortgage, then the second mortgagee moves into second place on the totem pole and you drop to third. Once a sale occurs, the first lender (mortgagee) still has priority to all money required to pay it out in full. Any excess then goes to the second mortgagee to pay it out in full. What's left, if anything, goes to you.

Similarly, if you place a third mortgage on that same property, the third mortgagee takes over third position on the totem pole and you slide down to fourth.

A third mortgage is nothing more than a third separate loan taken out using your property as security. It is registered third in time behind an existing first and an existing second mortgage.

As you can see, as a lender's position on the totem pole gets lower and lower, its risk gets higher and higher. Each mortgage registered on your property reduces the equity (cash value) in your home. The lenders in second or third position may be in a situation where the total amount of the mortgages ahead of them on the totem pole plus the face amount of their loan equals the fair market value of the property.

7

If the value of the property decreases, the lenders lower down on the totem pole may not be able to get their money back out of the property if a default occurs and a forced sale takes place. To take this extra risk, therefore, the second or third mortgage lender will want a greater return on its loan than the first mortgagee whose loan probably does not exceed 75% of the value of the property. The first lender accordingly has a built-in cushion to protect it even if values drop.

This greater return for the second or third lender usually takes the form of higher interest rates. Therefore, second mortgage rates are higher than first mortgage rates and third mortgage rates are even higher than second mortgage rates.

As you can see, only after all the lenders ahead of you on the totem pole are taken care of will there be any money left over for you. If you are simply valuing your property and not selling it, then the difference between the total amount of the mortgages ahead of you on the totem pole and the fair market value of the property is your equity in the house. The amount of equity in your house will become cash in your pocket if the property is actually sold for its fair market value.

Most of what is said in this book about obtaining mortgages and default under mortgages applies to second or third mortgages as well as to first mortgages.

## c. EQUITY: THE CASH VALUE OF YOUR HOUSE

This section discusses briefly the mysterious concept of "equity" and how it relates to mortgages. This equity differs from the equity associated with the courts of equity discussed earlier.

One of the first things that a lender looks at when deciding whether or not to make a mortgage loan is the value of the land that will form part of the security. An appraisal is made in order to determine a fair market value of the land.

Although appraisers are very highly skilled and well qualified, appraising is an art not a science. Evaluations are to some extent subjective. This means that the same piece of property can be appraised by two or three appraisers and different values obtained. However, most of the variations are within 5 or 10% of each other; over the years, lenders have built up confidence in the ability of appraisers to properly estimate fair market value for properties.

Once a valuation of the land has been made, the equity position of the owner (borrower) can be determined.

Equity basically refers to the value that the owner has in the property, or to put it another way, the difference between the fair market value of the property and the total amount of money still owed for that property.

For example, assume that Howse Buyer wants to buy a house. He has $30 000 in cash. He has found the house of his dreams. However, the price is $80 000. In order for Mr. Buyer to be able to buy the house, he will have to arrange a loan of $50 000. This loan will, of course, be a mortgage for that amount.

The $30 000 cash that Mr. Buyer will invest in the house represents his equity in the house. We can assume that $80 000 represented a fair market value for the house because Howse Buyer is an "arm's length" purchaser. An arm's length transaction is one where a sale results between a purchaser and a seller who bear no special duty or relation to each other.

The fair market value of the property is constantly changing; because it was bought for $80 000 at one point, it certainly does not mean that its value is frozen at that amount forever. In fact we all hope when we buy our houses that the value of the property will go up.

As the value of the property goes up, our equity position increases. For example, assume that the house was purchased by Mr. Buyer in 1978. At that time the fair market value was $80 000. Four years later, however, an appraisal of the property showed the fair market value to be $120 000. Assuming for a moment that the principal balance of the mortgage on the property has remained the same, that is $50 000, the equity that Mr. Buyer has in the property has increased from $30 000 to $70 000. This means that if he sold the property, he would actually receive $70 000 cash for an initial $30 000 investment.

On the other side of the coin, however, if the property goes down in value, then the equity decreases. Assume that the house was purchased for $80 000 in 1981. Given the economic turn down in 1982 it is feasible that the property would be appraised one year later at $70 000. This means that the equity of Mr. Buyer in the property was reduced from $30 000 to $20 000. If he sold the property at that time, he could only hope to receive $20 000 back from his initial $30 000 deposit, meaning a loss of $10 000. His equity position dropped. The lender's position is not affected at all.

Equity can also be affected by changes to the mortgage balance. For example, if the value of the property remained at $80 000 and Mr. Buyer was able to pay off half his mortgage loan, the equity in the property would jump from $30 000 to $55 000, which is the difference between the property value of $80 000 and the new mortgage balance of $25 000.

It is possible to take cash out of your property by the use of additional mortgages and decrease your equity position. For example, assume that Mr. Buyer decides to build a garage on his property and needs $10 000 cash. He could take out a second mortgage in the amount of $10 000 to be registered on his title. Assuming then that the property is still worth $80 000, Mr. Buyer would now have an equity of $20 000, the difference between the value of $80 000 and the total amount of the financing registered against the land, which is now $60 000.

The value of the property has remained the same and what Howse has done is simply converted $10 000 of his equity into cash to build the garage. The price that he paid for this right is that, although he received $10 000, he is going to have to repay it to the second lender with interest. If Howse repays the second mortgage in full within one year, his equity will then revert to the $30 000 mark that it was prior to the second mortgage being registered against the property.

Assume that one year after getting the $10 000 loan, Howse has some financial difficulties in his business and wants an additional $5 000. He could convert an additional

$5000 worth of equity in his property into cash, which would reduce his equity to $15000. He could do this by putting a third mortgage on the property for $5000.

The equity in property may also be used as security. For example, assume that Howse has a first mortgage on his property for $50000. Also assume that Howse has his own automotive business and because of tough times has a $20000 overdraft at the bank. Looking for a way to satisfy the bank and provide the bank with security so as to not endanger the business or cause a lawsuit, Howse pledges $20000 of his equity in his house to the bank in a second mortgage.

If Howse's business goes under and he has to sell his house, the bank ranks first in priority for repayment of its $20000 security after payment of the first $50000 mortgage. The bank could take the security of a second mortgage on Howse's home and allow him to retain the overdraft until it is paid.

So, you may use the equity in your house to convert it into cash or as security for debts or other obligations, or simply let it increase as an investment.

# 2

# YOUR OBLIGATIONS UNDER
# ANY MORTGAGE

Before talking about specific kinds of mortgages, I will explain what you must do to fulfil your obligations as a borrower under any kind of mortgage.

You are, in exchange for these obligations, entitled to possession of the land at all times during the mortgage term. Unless there is some special agreement between the parties, the lender is not entitled to possession and may not interfere with the borrower. For example, the lender is not entitled to collect rent on the property or to make repairs or other improvements to the property. This presupposes that you, as borrower, live up to your end of the mortgage agreement.

The obvious and most important obligation of the borrower is to make the payments that are owing under the mortgage. As discussed, the amount of the payment and where the payments are to be made are normally stated in the mortgage. In most cases, payments are required on the first day of each month and can often include, in addition to the normal payments under the mortgage, some additional payments for tax or insurance or other items.

It is the obligation of the borrower to ensure that those payments are delivered promptly and in the proper amounts to the lender. Many lenders include in their mortgage the requirement of post-dated cheques, and many lending institutions have made arrangements for a pre-authorized withdrawal system which allows money to be automatically withdrawn from the borrower's account on the due dates under the mortgage.

Because the mortgage is a contract, failure to make a payment on the day that it is due or in the amount required is technically a breach of the mortgage agreement. The severity of the breach will depend on the circumstances in each particular case. If, for example, mortgage payments are due once every five years in the amount of $20 000, failure to make the payment when required will be treated in a more serious light than if a monthly mortgage payment is short by $25. However, the effect of both is the same in that it can be deemed to be a default and legal consequences can result from the failure to make the proper payment.

Although the requirement for payment is the most important requirement, there are other ongoing obligations that must be complied with. Here is a list of some of the requirements that are found in most standard form residential mortgages:

(a) The borrower must comply with all laws, rules, and regulations affecting the mortgage premises, i.e., this might include the requirement that if a property is zoned only for single family residence, the borrower shall not put in an illegal suite in the basement.

(b) The borrower must maintain adequate insurance on the premises; this is a key form of protection for the mortgage lender. If there is a fire or other damage to the property, the lender wants to make sure that either the damage is repaired or the mortgage proceeds are paid to the lender.

(c) The borrower must make sure that all municipal or property taxes are paid; this again is an important requirement because if the property taxes are not paid; the property may be subject to sale by the regulating authority to cover outstanding taxes.

(d) The borrower must keep the property in good condition; the legal concept of preventing "waste" is found in most mortgages. This is a requirement that the borrower not allow any damage or destruction to the premises that would in any way affect the security of the lender. The borrower must repair all waste to ensure that the security remains in place.

13

(e) If the premises involve rental property, there is normally a clause in the mortgage requiring the borrower to ensure that all rents are collected in order that the mortgage payments can be met.

(f) The borrower may not sell the property without the consent of the lender. It is a default under a mortgage in most cases to sell premises to buyers who are going to assume the mortgage without obtaining the consent of the lender.

(g) Where there is a second or third mortgage on title, there is normally a requirement in it that the borrower ensure that the previous mortgages are kept in good standing. Therefore, a default in payment under a first mortgage could amount to a default under the second mortgage even if all of the payments under the second mortgage have been kept up.

(h) The borrower has responsibility for all costs associated with the mortgage; these include the initial legal fees and disbursements involved in setting up the mortgage as well as all of the subsequent costs that might be involved in renewals to the mortgage or any costs incurred by the lender in a default under the mortgage. Those costs are discussed later.

The lender may begin legal action on the basis of any of the above defaults, so it is extremely important to understand your duties under the mortgage and to fulfil them.

# 3

# TYPES OF MORTGAGES

This chapter will provide a short description of the main types of mortgages that are currently available. Depending on the type of mortgage you have, your rights and the lender's may differ. In every instance, however, you are involved in a contract that sets out the rights of the parties.

## a. THE CONVENTIONAL MORTGAGE
The conventional mortgage is by far the most common type of mortgage on residential premises. It provides for the basic mortgage loan secured by the borrower's interest in certain property. The term "conventional" is used because it is the standard model of lending agreements. Just as automakers sometimes refer to their standard vehicles as conventional models, lenders have created a basic agreement. If there are fancy accessories or modifications to the automobile, it is no longer the conventional model and is renamed. Similarly, a mortgage that contains additional clauses or is designed to cover special purposes is known as an unconventional mortgage and is normally renamed.

The conventional mortgage contains all of the basic terms discussed earlier, including the obligations of the parties.

Conventional mortgages are available from banks and trust companies. They will normally provide loans of up to 75% of the appraised value of the property and, in most cases, for residential purposes only.

## b. INSURED MORTGAGES
Borrowers are required to put up a substantial amount of a cash down payment in order to qualify for the mortgage.

15

This is normally known as a "low ratio" mortgage because the ratio of the mortgage to the full value of the property is low, i.e., 75% or even lower in some provinces.

However, in the 1950s, the government recognized that there was a fairly large demand for higher ratio mortgages because individuals simply could not put down 25% or more of the purchase price. Accordingly, the concept of insurable mortgages arose. This means that the lender can obtain insurance from some source, either public or private, that protects it in a default by the borrower. Because of this protection, the lender can make a higher ratio loan of up to 90% and sometimes even 95% of the value of the property.

The benefit to the borrower is obvious: he or she does not have to put up a great deal of cash in order to acquire the property. The benefit to the lender is also obvious: the lender can make a substantial number of mortgage loans and, theoretically, a substantial profit.

Mortgage insurance can be obtained either publicly or privately. Public insurance is obtained from the Canada Mortgage and Housing Corporation (usually known as CMHC). This is a federally financed program. It provides an avenue through which federal policies affecting housing can be introduced into the marketplace, and it is designed to provide some overall long-term stability and control in that aspect of the Canadian economy. The banks, however, still administer the mortgage.

The essential requirements of a CMHC loan are that the housing be intended for full-time occupancy, that it meet or be capable of meeting prescribed construction standards, and that the borrower not spend more than a reasonable proportion (generally 30%) of gross income for mortgage and tax payments.

The "premium" or price for this insurance is collected at the time of the mortgage advance. These premiums form the pool of funds that are available to lenders in a default.

Although the lender is theoretically responsible for making the premium payment to the mortgage company, in fact, this amount is added to the principal amount of the mortgage. The premium normally amounts to 1 to 2½% of the loan amount.

The largest private insurer in Canada is the Mortgage Insurance Company of Canada, commonly known as MICC. This company came into being in November, 1981, as a result of an amalgamation of the Mortgage Insurance Company of Canada and Insmore Mortgage Insurance Company. It is a private company that provides funding and, like CMHC, imposes certain requirements on borrowers before it will insure a loan. Those requirements are based to a large extent on the construction aspects of the property involved and the type of building on the land. However, MICC mortgages normally cover loans not covered under CMHC financing.

Recently, more than two-thirds of all mortgage commitments that were issued one year were for insured mortgages.

In addition to the insurance coverage that MICC and CMHC provide, they offer a considerable amount of back-up assistance to the lender. They maintain appraisal and inspection divisions throughout Canada. They have staff who can assist lenders in deciding whether or not to make a loan.

Under private mortgage insurance, lenders can follow their own policies and procedures, use their own forms, have their mortgage insured without a lot of government red tape, and receive immediate service. Under government insurance, the lender must follow the special procedures laid down by CMHC.

The fact that a mortgage is insured may be significant when a borrower has defaulted on the mortgage. If the mortgage is insured and the lender is satisfied that it cannot recover its money from the borrower, it can always claim for the loss under its insurance with either MICC or CMHC. The lender may not be as co-operative with a mortgagor who wants to refinance the loan, reschedule the debt or even quit claim the interest back to the lender. Each lender approaches these situations differently, and no generalizations should be accepted as gospel.

The mortgage contract itself is similar to the conventional mortgage in its terms and conditions. The major difference is in the additional back-up protection it provides to the lender and the special clauses inserted in the agreement as part of the insurance coverage.

## c. AGREEMENT FOR SALE

An agreement for sale is an alternative to a mortgage. It is used in a situation where the buyer of the property does not make a large down payment. The parties to an agreement for sale are the purchaser and the vendor (seller) of the property. This is different from a mortgage where the parties to the mortgage may not necessarily be the purchaser and the vendor (see discussion on vendor take-back mortgages below) and, in fact, the lender is usually a third party.

In a normal mortgage situation A buys the property from B and arranges a mortgage with C to help complete the purchase. Under an agreement for sale, A buys the property from B and B provides all or most of the financing for the purchase.

A purchaser under an agreement for sale does not become the legal owner of the property until payments to the vendor have reached an agreed stage at which time the purchaser becomes entitled to a conveyance of the legal interest.

When the agreement is first made, the purchaser under an agreement for sale has an "equitable interest" in the property. After complying with the terms of the agreement for sale, the purchaser is entitled to become the registered or legal owner of the property.

In addition, the purchaser and the vendor will enter into a contract that contains many terms similar to the terms found in a mortgage. The agreement will also contain the rules and procedures governing the rights of the parties and particularly the obligations of the parties regarding the payment of the money the purchaser owes the vendor.

The agreement for sale is a useful tool available to purchasers who do not wish to arrange separate financing with a mortgage company. It saves the initial mortgage costs of application fees, appraisal fees, and legal costs.

Today, it is used in cases where the purchaser cannot qualify to assume the existing mortgage. By entering into this type of arrangement, a purchaser can in effect assume a mortgage that would otherwise be unavailable.

It works like this. Assume Johnny Buyer wants to buy Vera Vendor's home. Vera's house is on sale for $100 000 and is subject to an $80 000 first mortgage. Johnny has the necessary $20 000, but because he has recently been unemployed, there is no way that he can qualify for the mortgage.

Although in most cases the mortgage would be automatically assumable, let us suppose that in this case, the mortgage is a "collateral" mortgage (see page 23) and not assumable.

Under an agreement for sale, title to the property stays in Vera Vendor's name, Johnny pays the $20 000 to Vera and protects his interest on title by registering some type of claim against the title. Johnny is then obligated to make mortgage payments to Vera who in turn pays her lender. As far as the lender is concerned, Vera is its borrower and she is held responsible for the payments. Vera, of course, looks to Johnny for payment. Even if Johnny does not pay her, Vera is still obliged to pay her lender. Once the mortgage term expires, Johnny is normally required to pay off Vera's mortgage at which time he will get title to the property.

If the purchaser fails to make payments, the remedies available to a lender are different in some instances from the remedies available to a vendor under an agreement for sale. For example, in British Columbia, the redemption period under an agreement for sale is normally three months while a redemption period in a mortgage situation is normally six months. A vendor under an agreement for sale may begin a legal action for specific performance and cancellation of the agreement, while the main remedy available to a lender is an action for foreclosure.

However, it is safe to say that in most cases the contract between the vendor and the purchaser will contain almost the identical clauses as in a normal mortgage agreement.

This puts the vendor in the position of a lender and the purchaser in the position of borrower.

## d. VENDOR TAKE-BACK MORTGAGES

The vendor take-back mortgage is, unlike the agreement for sale, an actual mortgage agreement between the purchaser and the vendor. Under the vendor take-back mortgage, the title to the property is transferred from the vendor to the purchaser. The vendor, in effect, takes the place of the third party mortgagee.

The vendor take-back mortgage is more common as a second or third mortgage rather than as a first mortgage. Often a purchaser wishes to buy property from a vendor and the property is already subject to an existing mortgage from a third party lender. Because the purchaser does not have enough cash, the vendor agrees to postpone payment of some or all of this cash difference in return for security on the property in the form of a mortgage.

For example, assume that Konrad Kastle is the owner of property worth $100 000. The property already has on it a mortgage from the Bigg Bank for $50 000. Paul Price wishes to purchase the property but only has $30 000 cash. With Mr. Price assuming the first mortgage to the Bigg Bank of $50 000 plus his $30 000 cash, he is still going to be $20 000 short. Mr. Kastle, recognizing that buyers these days are few and far between, agrees to defer payment to him of the additional $20 000 by agreeing to take it over a period of three years with 15% interest on the amount. The agreement is secured by way of a vendor take-back mortgage which the parties register on title after the interest of the Bigg Bank.

After the transaction has been completed, the property is subject to a first mortgage from the Bigg Bank in the amount of $50 000 and a second mortgage from Mr. Kastle for $20 000 with Paul Price as the proud owner.

If Paul Price defaults on his payments to Konrad Kastle, Mr. Kastle will have available to him all of the remedies that a lender bank has. Despite the fact that Mr. Kastle was the original vendor of the property, his rights as a lender will be the same as the rights of any other lender.

# e. WRAP-AROUND MORTGAGES

This type of mortgage has become popular in the last several years because of inflation and increasing interest rates. In order for a wrap-around mortgage to work, there must be a prior mortgage on a property that for one reason or another is not assumable.

The wrap-around mortgage is usually used when the purchaser wishes to take advantage of the benefits of an attractive existing mortgage. The lender (who is normally the vendor) is prepared to use this form of financing because of the additional benefit of receiving interest payments.

For example, assume that Hal Hunter wants to buy property from Olive Price. Price is selling the property for $140 000. The property is subject to a $70 000 first mortgage at 6%. The mortgage has 10 years remaining. Naturally, Hunter would like to retain that mortgage but simply does not have enough cash to complete the purchase. He only has $20 000 cash and, therefore, needs a $50 000 mortgage, in addition to the $70 000 mortgage already on the property.

One possibility is for Hunter simply to obtain a second mortgage for $50 000. Another possibility is for Price to carry the difference by way of a vendor take-back. The third choice is for Mr. Hunter to obtain a wrap-around mortgage for $120 000 which would "wrap-around" the first mortgage in order to take advantage of its favorable terms.

Mr. Hunter may be able to obtain a wrap-around mortgage of 14% for $120 000. If he wanted to obtain a second mortgage for $50 000, he would probably have to pay interest in the area of 17% or 18%. Therefore, the total payments would be considerably higher than the payments under a wrap-around mortgage.

A lender would be prepared to lend at 14% because not only would the lender be making 14% on the $50 000 but would be entitled to 14% on the full amount of the $120 000. It would be the "new" lender's responsibility to make the payments due on the first mortgage, but it would then be entitled to keep the difference between the 14%

and the 6% to be paid out on the existing first mortgage. This is the main benefit to the lender. In addition, the new lender has total control of the mortgage security.

There is another use for the wrap-around mortgage. There may be instances where the existing first mortgage on the property is not assumable because the mortgage is a collateral or blanket mortgage. However, the purchaser wants to retain that mortgage because it does provide some financing on the property. In order to retain this type of financing, a wrap-around mortgage can be used which will "wrap-around" the existing mortgage and also provide additional financing required to complete the transaction. The scenario is virtually the same as in the example above except that in this case, it is desirable to retain the first mortgage not so much because of a low interest rate or high principal balance but simply because the purchaser does not have the ability to obtain a mortgage any other way. As you may have noted, this is really a combination of an agreement for sale and a vendor take-back mortgage.

In both instances, the buyer makes payments to the wrap-around lender who in turn makes any payments that are due on the prior mortgage. Naturally, the wrap-around mortgage agreement has to have, as well as the normal clauses, additional clauses to protect the new lender.

They include:

(a) Clauses that are in the first mortgage so that the requirements under both are identical

(b) A clause indicating that the wrap-around mortgage lender is not obligated to make any payments to the existing first lender until the wrap-around mortgage lender has received all of its payments from the borrower

(c) A clause indicating that a default in payment to the first mortgage is a default in payment under the wrap-around mortgage

(d) A clause indicating that all notices on the first mortgage about default must go to the wrap-around mortgagee

(e) A restriction on the right to prepay the wrap-around mortgage

If there is a default of the first mortgage, the wrap-around mortgage lender would have the right to declare its mortgage in default as well and use any remedies available. Alternatively, a wrap-around mortgage lender could remedy the default under the first mortgage by making whatever payments are owing, and then adding that amount to the principal of the wrap-around portion of the wrap-around mortgage.

A default in the payments under the wrap-around mortgage again would result in a wrap-around lender having all of the usual remedies available to it.

## f. COLLATERAL MORTGAGES

Unlike the conventional mortgage, in which the mortgage really is the only security, a collateral mortgage normally is part of a lending package that involves additional forms of security required by the lender. These forms of security could include promissory notes, personal guarantees, assignments or other forms of security that may be required by a lender.

"Collateral" means that the mortgage security is actually collateral or secondary to some other prime form of security taken by the lender. In most cases, this prime security document will be a promissory note where the borrower has agreed in writing to repay the lender according to the terms of the note. However, as additional security, the lender requires the borrower to provide a mortgage on some land. The payment requirements are in the promissory note. If the promissory note is paid off by the borrower, the collateral security (the mortgage) will automatically be deemed to have been paid off and the borrower will be entitled to have the collateral mortgage discharged from the title.

As far as the mortgage itself is concerned, in addition to the usual clauses found in most mortgages, it contains a clause specifying that it is a collateral mortgage only and also indicates exactly what security the mortgage is collateral to. The terms of the collateral mortgage must be the same as the terms of the prime security instrument.

One of the important differences between a collateral mortgage and a conventional mortgage is the assumability of the collateral mortgage. There are some provinces where even though the mortgage contains a clause saying that the mortgage will not be assumed, the courts have held that the mortgage is assumable. This is not the case with a collateral mortgage. If the mortgage is collateral, then by definition it is subject to some other security between the parties. If the lender finds that the borrower is attempting to sell the secured property with the new purchaser assuming the mortgage, the lender is entitled to receive the whole balance owing under the mortgage or exercise other available remedies.

Other than that difference, the terms of the collateral mortgage will in all likelihood be very similar to the terms found in a conventional mortgage.

## g. VARIABLE INTEREST RATE MORTGAGES

Until very recently, all mortgages were set up with a fixed rate of interest over the term of the mortgage. In other words, whatever the rate was at the beginning of the term, it remained the same throughout the entire term of the loan.

However, because of rapidly fluctuating interest rates, the variable rate mortgage has become more popular. This mortgage is identical to other mortgages except that the interest rate varies or fluctuates according to some formula agreed to between the lender and borrower. The formula is normally based on the prime rate set each week by the Bank of Canada. Accordingly, the rate effectively varies from week to week as the Bank of Canada changes the prime rate.

In most cases, the mortgage payments are fixed. Obvious problems might arise if a person had to vary the mortgage payments monthly. The effect of this is that depending on the interest rate at any particular time, more or less of the cash payment made by the borrower is paid toward interest.

One of the potential dangers of a floating interest rate is that the interest rate could rise to a point where the monthly mortgage payment does not cover all of the interest; the borrower could fall into arrears without even knowing about it. Then, either the mortgage payment would have to be increased or the amounts unpaid would have to be added to the principal.

The remedies that are available to a lender are the same as under the conventional mortgage. The lender will, however, have to be exceedingly careful in determining the amount of the arrears.

There are many types of variable rate mortgages available. They range from basic floating mortgages that are tied to the Bank of Canada rate to mortgages that build in an increase in the interest rate with each passing year. You should check each one thoroughly before committing yourself to a mortgage of this type.

A recent innovation in both variable and fixed rate mortgages are those that are paid weekly, not monthly. This might assist homeowners who would prefer to make payments on a weekly basis in smaller amounts. Potential borrowers should investigate these mortgages thoroughly.

## h. CHATTEL MORTGAGES

Many people have the mistaken belief that the word "mortgage" always relates to land. This is not the case. As discussed earlier, a mortgage is really a contract between two parties. A chattel mortgage is a contract between two parties using as security assets that are known as chattels. These are basically items of personal property, not land, and include motor vehicles, equipment or machinery.

The terms of a chattel mortgage are quite similar to the terms of a land mortgage. However, the registration requirements and certain of the remedies are quite different. Chattel mortgages are mentioned here only so that you can distinguish them from land mortgages.

# i. BLANKET MORTGAGES

A blanket mortgage is a mortgage registered over two or more properties. The idea behind it is to provide the lender with more than one piece of land as security.

For example, assume that you wish to buy a home for $100 000 with a $10 000 down payment and the balance by mortgage. Most lenders are reluctant to lend to the value of 90% of the purchase price for the reasons discussed earlier. However, if you happened to own another piece of property with $100 000 clear title, a lender may be prepared to loan you $90 000 if you allowed both properties to be mortgaged.

The lender would take a blanket mortgage over both properties securing $90 000 on each one. Both properties are tied up until the loan is repaid, meaning that you cannot sell or mortgage either property without taking the $90 000 mortgage into consideration.

Naturally, the lender is only entitled to be repaid the original loan plus interest. It is not entitled to $90 000 from each property.

A blanket mortgage can be based on any type of mortgage already discussed. It will contain a special clause identifying it as securing two or more properties. Therefore, the remedies available to a lender are based on the normal remedies available under any mortgage. However, if default occurs, the lender can choose which property to proceed against and, in fact, can proceed against both. If the sale of one property does not satisfy the debt, the second will then be sold.

# j. MORTGAGES ON UNDIVIDED INTERESTS OF PROPERTY

This book is basically restricted to discussing mortgages on residential property. Although the vast majority of mortgages on residential property will bind the entire legal interest on the property, there are situations where this may not apply.

Most residential properties are owned by a husband and wife in joint tenancy. This means that the property is owned by both spouses and that it is deemed to be transferred to the surviving spouse just prior to the death of the other. The effect of this transfer is that the property does not go into the estate of the deceased; it allows the surviving spouse the immediate benefits of ownership.

The second most common way that a husband and wife own a house is in a tenancy in common. With tenancy in common, both parties are deemed to be owners of the full legal interest in the property. However, the difference between a tenancy in common and a joint tenancy is that when one spouse dies, the property is not automatically transferred to the surviving spouse. The property is dealt with like any other asset of the deceased and, therefore, it passes to the deceased's estate.

In most situations, because the surviving spouse will probably be the beneficiary under the will, the surviving spouse will end up with the property; but if the property is held in tenancy in common, the deceased's will or the rules for the administration of estates (if there is no will), must confirm this.

In both the above situations, the mortgage is registered against the entire legal interest on the property. This means that both the husband and the wife have signed the mortgage documents and are named as parties in a mortgage action. If the property is sold or some other remedy is obtained, it will affect the entire property and both parties' interest in it.

An example will illustrate this particular problem. Assume that Mr. and Mrs. Equity hold a property jointly and each contributes half of the mortgage payment. If Mr. Equity continues to make his mortgage payments, but Mrs. Equity does not because she lost her job, the entire mortgage will be behind in payments. It is not a defence for Mr. Equity to say that because he is making his mortgage payments, the action on the mortgage should not affect him. Because of the way that the title is held, the mortgage company is able to take action against the entire property.

The third way of holding property is as an undivided interest. This is quite an unusual way of holding property between spouses, but when people who are not married are doubling up to acquire accommodation they may not want the property to automatically transfer to the survivor after death. In addition, the individuals holding the property may want to be able to freely sell their half of the property without requiring the consent of the other. In order to accomplish this, the property can be held as an undivided 50% interest. This means that each party owns a 50% interest in the land and is free to sell that interest without getting the consent of the other party. In addition, each party is entitled to mortgage his or her half of the property without the consent of the other party.

The effect of this is that a mortgage action against one party's undivided interest would not affect the other party's undivided interest or the mortgage held by that other party. See chapter 12 for an example of how this works.

These types of mortgages may become more and more common in the 1980s. The major difficulty will be finding a mortgage lender who is prepared to lend money on an undivided interest in land. In all likelihood this mortgage will have to be an insured mortgage, but recent developments indicate that lenders may be more willing to lend on this basis in the future.

## k. CONDOMINIUM MORTGAGES

Many people these days are buying or living in condominiums. Just like buying a house, however, unless the condominium is purchased for cash, it is necessary to obtain a loan to pay for it. Condominium mortgages are very common now and, except for a few special provisions, are very similar to the other types of mortgages discussed.

Each purchaser of a condominium receives a legal title to one individual unit plus some form of undivided interest in the common area.

The first mortgage registered against the entire condominium project is a blanket mortgage. This is, as already discussed, a mortgage blanketing all of the individual units and the common areas. The blanket mortgage is normally placed on the project by the developer, who uses the funds from the blanket mortgage to construct the project. As individual units are sold, the blanket mortgage is then discharged off the sold units and, in return, you as the purchaser place your own condominium mortgage on your title.

This mortgage contains most of the terms already discussed. In addition, however, the mortgage contains a few clauses especially related to condominiums.

The most important of the unique features in a condominium mortgage gives the unit lender the right to use the unit owner's vote or consent in the condominium corporation. In other words, the lender, and not the owner, is entitled to a vote in the condominium corporation. The corporation operates and manages the condominium complex. In practice, the lender does not usually vote on all decisions or on all occasions, although the borrower is obligated to provide notice of all condominium corporation meetings and all other information received from the condominium corporation.

Another unique feature found in the condominium unit mortgage is a provision allowing the lender to pay the common area costs if you fail to do so. Naturally these costs are then added to the principal amount of the mortgage to be repaid with interest.

Finally, the lender includes in the mortgage the right to demand that the borrower comply with all the terms of the condominium by-laws. Thus, if you breach any of the condominium by-laws, you will be defaulting under your mortgage.

The obligations you have as a condominium owner are slightly more onerous as far as the mortgage is concerned. This is mainly because of the legal nature of the condominium.

# 4

## APPLYING FOR A MORTGAGE

This chapter discusses how best to apply for and obtain a mortgage. The application process can be a trying and frustrating time for young people attempting to arrange for a first loan. Depending on how you apply, the application procedure can be accomplished quickly and successfully.

## a. THE INFORMATION NEEDED

The two most important pieces of information that a lender requires is information about your personal financial situation and information about the property that you are buying.

Each lender has its own application form and requires specific types of information. However, in all situations the lender requires the following information.

### 1. The loan — vital details

The lender obviously wants information about why the loan is required (probably either for a purchase or a re-finance of a property), the amount of the loan (the amount of money you need), the term of loan that you want, the interest rate that you are applying for, and any special conditions in the mortgage as required.

### 2. Financial information

The potential lender wants a full credit report on you. This will either be supplied by you or by other sources and, on some occasions, by both. You must provide the lender with full information about your job history, existing income, income of your spouse, age, address, and the various sources of income available to you in order to verify that you have the ability to make the mortgage payments.

In addition, it is always a good idea to provide the potential mortgagee with two additional statements. One statement is the equivalent of a balance statement that a company prepares each year. For an individual, the statement is known as a "net worth" statement. It gives the lender an idea of the total picture of your assets and liabilities at the time of your application.

The second statement is an income statement, which indicates the amount of your income and the sources of this income. This gives the lender an idea about how the mortgage will be paid.

Most lenders require verification of employment income from the employer. You can get this simply by obtaining a letter from your employer. In addition, it may be necessary to provide similar verification from third parties depending on the circumstances. For example, if the money to pay for the mortgage payments will be coming out of the interest earned on Canada Savings Bonds or term deposits that are held at a bank, verification from the bank where the bonds or deposits are kept will be required.

### 3. Details about the property

It is important to give the potential lender full details about the property.

The information that you should provide includes a legal description of the property, a copy of the listing agreement, the civic address, a general description of the property, the offer to purchase, and a surveyor's certificate or appraisal of the property if available. Any information that can be given at this time will save a considerable amount of time when it comes to obtaining the approval.

The mortgage application form is a disclosure statement that by law requires full and complete disclosure by you as mortgagor. Any omission or deliberate falsehood in the statement may result in a mortgagee taking action on the mortgage once the problem is discovered — even if the loan itself is in good standing. When you sign the application form, you are saying to the potential lender that all the information you have given is true and accurate.

You should also note that as part of the application you are usually committing yourself to pay the costs involved in the preparation of the mortgage. These include all of the application fees, the appraisal costs, and the legal fees and disbursements involved in the preparation and registration of the mortgage. This amount can be rather significant and, when applying for the mortgage, you should always obtain a detailed breakdown of those costs so that you know beforehand what they will be. These costs, especially the legal fees, are almost always negotiable.

Once the application is taken, the lender will attempt to verify the information by running a detailed credit analysis of the personal information you have given.

In addition, the lender will require some verification of the value of the property, usually by an appraisal. For a mortgage, the appraiser looks at the property to see if either the purchase price or the refinancing value is justified. Unless the circumstances are quite unusual, the appraisal of the property will fall into a range that is acceptable to the lender. The usual rule of thumb is that a conventional lender will loan up to 75% of the appraised value. A "high risk" lender will often go as high as 85% or 95% but may charge a higher interest rate, a bonus fee or both.

Although you pay for the appraisal, quite often the appraiser sends the report directly to the lender. You are entitled to review the appraisal because you paid for it; ask the appraiser directly or the lender for a copy of the appraisal report.

Any information that you can provide to the appraiser to help justify the value will be of assistance. It is often necessary to obtain the co-operation of the owner of the property to ensure that the appraiser gets a good look at the premises and is made aware of all of the improvements on it.

Mortgage applications can be made directly to a lender or through an intermediary known as a mortgage broker. A mortgage broker is an individual or company involved in the business of arranging mortgages. A mortgage broker takes a fee, amounting to a percentage of the actual mortgage, as remuneration. In return, the broker takes the information from you and locates a lender on your behalf.

A mortgage broker is of benefit when you have absolutely no expertise or no desire to apply yourself or when you may have problems qualifying for the loan. A broker has available sources who would make the loan and who would not be available to you.

Brokers are particularly beneficial if you have had problems in the past with bad debts, foreclosures, and the like. Although you will pay a brokerage fee and perhaps an additional bonus to the lender or a higher rate of interest, it may be worth it to you in the long run.

Most brokers are respectable and knowledgeable in the realm of borrowing and lending money. They maintain professional standards and are governed by laws in each province. A broker must disclose in writing to a borrower, before the borrower actually signs the mortgage papers, all the costs and deductions associated with the loan.

If you wish to locate a broker to assist you in arranging a loan, my advice is to contact your local Mortgage Broker Association. They will recommend brokers who have expertise in obtaining mortgage loans for the particular type of property and loan involved.

The above information represents those things that you must think about and provide for when you are applying for a mortgage for your own residence. There are a number of other considerations involved in borrowing money for commercial or investment properties, but they are beyond the scope of this book. Further information can be obtained free by asking a mortgage broker what information is required before he or she can arrange a mortgage for you.

For purposes of residential mortgages, however, the key element is the credit information that you provide about yourself and the information about the property. As long as the property values hold up and you are personally in a position to "service the debt" (make the monthly mortgage payments), with the proper verifications, you should be able to obtain the loan.

## b. TIPS ON FINDING A MORTGAGE

### 1. Shop around for the best interest rates

Whether you are refinancing or placing a new mortgage on the property, you will soon find that companies offer differing rates. Insurance companies, credit unions, and pension funds often offer the best rates but qualification requirements may be more difficult to meet.

Banks and trust companies have large quantities of money available for loan purposes but have rates slightly higher than insurance companies, credit unions, and pension funds.

Private lenders form a third group of potential mortgagees. Their rates are traditionally higher but they may qualify you when other lenders will not.

Mortgage interest rates also vary depending on the term of the mortgage, the position of the mortgagee on title (first, second or third), the equity and value of the property, and your credit rating. Remember to take into consideration any subsidy program that your provincial government may offer.

### 2. Fixed or floating rate?

You have a choice of obtaining a mortgage with either a fixed or a floating interest rate. A fixed rate means that the interest rate remains the same throughout the term of the mortgage. With a floating rate, your rate fluctuates based on the movements of the Bank of Canada rate. Which is better?

If you think that the rates will drop in the future, a floating rate is preferable. However, if you anticipate a rise in the rates during the mortgage term, then go for a fixed rate. In most cases, you are paying your mortgage payment with "after-tax" dollars meaning that you cannot write off your payments.

Gamblers will choose the floating rate of interest. If you are conservative and prudent, however, fix your mortgage rate. It may be higher than the rates next year but you will have some certainty in knowing what your payments will be throughout the mortgage term. This will allow you to properly budget your expenses over a period of time.

A fixed rate, coupled with an "open" mortgage (discussed below) will provide you with the best of both worlds.

### 3. Open mortgage

If you can obtain an open mortgage — all other things being equal — grab it! An open mortgage allows you a great deal of flexibility. You can prepay it whenever you want, but the lender is stuck with its terms. If the rate is low, and the term extended, the lender cannot do anything about it. If the interest rate is higher than the going rates, you can always refinance the property at a lower rate without any problem.

A closed mortgage restricts your choices and locks you into its terms. If the rates are high, you will be stuck with those payments.

Unfortunately, the open mortgage is rapidly becoming a thing of the past because lenders have become aware of its disadvantages for them. If you can find a three year or more open mortgage with a competitive interest rate, it is a desirable investment. See chapter 5 for more information.

### 4. Long term or short term?

Again, the choice of a mortgage term is a decision based on individual preference. Some people want a short term so that they will not be bound by onerous mortgage terms for a long period of time.

A longer mortgage term provides security if you are concerned about your ability to refinance once the existing mortgage expires and want to do some long range budgeting and planning.

If the mortgage is closed, a shorter term may be desirable. If there is a possibility that in the near future, you will be able to come up with a substantial payment that you can use for your mortgage, choose a short term mortgage.

With an open mortgage, however, my advice is to get the longest term possible. In this way, you maximize your advantages. Although you can "tie-in" the terms of the mortgage for the long term, if rates improve, you can pay off all or a portion of the mortgage. You (and not the mortgagee) can terminate the mortgage agreement and obtain a new one with more favorable terms.

### 5. Prepayment

As noted earlier, if you keep a mortgage for its full amortization period, you will probably pay four or five dollars interest for every dollar of principal you pay. It follows that the faster you can pay off your principal balance, the less interest you will pay in the long run.

Because mortgage payments are structured to pay interest first and then principal, almost all of your payment over the first years is interest. In order for you to reduce your principal you have to make payments in addition to your monthly payments.

Whatever you can scrape together to pay on your mortgage — do it! Remember, that if your mortgage is locked in, you will not be able to pay anything down on your principal. (This, of course, is another reason why an open mortgage is preferable.)

Although you may not be able to find a mortgage that is completely open, the next best thing is to find a mortgage that is partially open. This means that you will at least be able to pay a portion (normally 10%) of your principal each year. This will at least reduce the principal owing and also increase the principal portion of your monthly mortgage payment. Also, by reducing the amortization period, you will, in the long run, save on interest payments.

Some mortgages now allow for weekly, rather than monthly, payments. Weekly payments are designed to reduce the principal more quickly than monthly payments.

## 6. Size of the mortgage

The size of the mortgage is probably the single most important decision you have to make. Should you "lever" yourself as much as possible and arrange for the largest mortgage available, or should you be ultra-conservative and keep your borrowing to a minimum?

Your personal investment strategy will play a major role in your decision. If you believe in using someone else's money to finance your house, you'll go for the large loan. If you do not believe in borrowing money, then in all likelihood this will carry over into your thinking about mortgages.

Unlike other investments, you probably will not be able to write off your interest as an expense against your personal income. Therefore, the advantage of borrowing large amounts for the write-off simply does not exist.

You must also look at your ability to handle a large mortgage loan. It is really quite foolish to borrow a large amount and not be able to make the payments. All that will happen is that you will lose whatever equity you have put into the property that much faster.

Another consideration is the condition of the market at the time of the loan. In a rising market, a larger mortgage might be safer because your equity will increase and provide you with a cushion if you fall temporarily into default.

With a falling market, however, the more cash you put in, the more of a safety zone you will have if your equity begins to erode.

## 7. New options

Ever-increasing competition among mortgage lenders means the options available for potential borrowers have never been better. The various packages available are extensive and include some of the following options not normally granted on mortgage loans:

(a) The option to pay, either once a year or monthly, at your option, an amount over and above your normal monthly mortgage payment. You can pay an additional 15%, 20% or even 100% of your monthly payment. This "doubling up" right effectively means that all the extra money is being applied to reduce your principal, which will ultimately save you hundreds or thousands of dollars in interest.

(b) The option to make an annual one-time lump sum principal reduction of any amount at any time during the mortgage year. Many mortgages allow you to pay off 10% of the mortgage on the anniversary date, but this option allows you an opportunity at any time during the mortgage year to make a substantial reduction of your principal based on the amount of money you can afford to pay in any one year.

(c) The option to prepay your mortgage at any time, if the interest rate of your mortgage at the time of the proposed payout is equal to or greater than the rate of the mortgage. Mortgage companies are prepared to let you out of your mortgage if they can put that money to use at a higher return to them. You should consider this option only if it would not be necessary to refinance your mortgage, because you effectively would be refinancing at a higher rate. You should also be aware of the various requirements lenders impose in allowing you to pay out the mortgage. If the lender attempts to charge you a bonus payment of any type, or an amount equal to what you would otherwise have paid under the mortgage (known as the interest differential), there is really no benefit in paying out your mortgage because all you would be doing is prepaying the interest.

(d) The option to transfer your mortgage to another home. This allows you to purchase another house and automatically (subject to some preconditions imposed by the lender when you take out the mortgage originally) place a mortgage on the new house with a principal value equal to and sometimes even greater than the principal value of the mortgage on your old house. The advantage to you is that you do not have to go through the process of qualifying for the new mortgage. If financial conditions are such that you might not otherwise qualify, or if the value of the new house wouldn't justify the amount you are seeking, this can be a life-saver for you.

(e) The option to lock in an interest rate if you have a variable rate interest mortgage. If your mortgage interest rate fluctuates with the prime rate, your mortgage may give you the right to fix your interest rate at any time during the term of the mortgage. Therefore, if interest rates are about to go up, and fixed mortgage rates at that time are at a level you can afford, check your mortgage to see if it allows you, on a one-time basis, to give notice to the mortgage company of your intention to fix your interest at current rates. For the remaining term under your mortgage, your rate will be fixed at the rate you select. If the prime rate drops, you may ultimately pay more interest, but if the rate goes up, you may end up a big winner.

(f) The option to automatically renew your mortgage. As discussed elsewhere in this book, normally the lender decides whether to renew your mortgage once the term has expired. However, in certain instances, the lender will allow you, at your sole option, to renew the mortgage. This right usually exists when there are a number of years left on the mortgage term. There may be other preconditions involved in the renewal such as ensuring that the interest rate of your mortgage is at least equal to current mortgage interest rates at the time you exercise your right to renew. No matter what the conditions are, this right can be of tremendous advantage to you. It allows you to gain security by extending the mortgage term under conditions satisfactory to you. You need not worry about the lender calling in the loan at the expiration of the mortgage term. It avoids the problems associated with having to locate a new mortgage.

(g) The option to transfer your mortgage to another mortgage lender. Many lenders, especially banks, who are eager for mortgage business, will now allow you to transfer your existing mortgage to them when it is up for renewal. The cost is nominal to you and there may be long-term benefits for you if you switch. For example, if another lender provides a more liberal prepayment option, it would pay to switch over.

## c. GOVERNMENT ASSISTANCE FOR BORROWERS

In response to the high interest rates of mortgages taken out or renewed in 1980 and 1981 and the resulting hardship on borrowers, the federal government and some provincial governments provided mortgage relief or subsidy programs. Most programs provided a subsidy by way of grant or loan to qualified homeowners to cover a portion of their mortgage payments. These programs were very popular in British Columbia, Alberta, Saskatchewan, and Manitoba. At the time of publication, most of these programs had expired or were about to expire.

It may be that one or more of the provinces will renew or revise their mortgage assistance programs. This will depend on the fluctuation in interest rates and how many people require assistance. If you are currently taking advantage of a provincial assistance program, contact the local provincial government office in your area to determine what benefits may be available in assisting you with your mortgage payments in the future.

Federally, a mortgage insurance program is available which is discussed in the next chapter. Also, CMHC has a plan to assist homeowners with renewals if your payments exceed 30% of your gross income. Contact your local CMHC office for details.

# 5

# RENEWING OR PREPAYING
# YOUR MORTGAGE

## a. RENEWING YOUR MORTGAGE

The contract term of a mortgage is normally set for a period of up to five years. What happens when the mortgage term ends?

Many people think a lender is obligated in some legal way to automatically renew the mortgage agreement. This is not the case. Once the contract has expired, the lender is entitled to demand full payment of the principal. If you fail to pay the money owed, the lender can begin legal action.

The other option open to the lender is to enter into a new agreement with the borrower. This new arrangement is a renewal agreement. The renewal agreement normally provides that the lender will continue to allow the borrower to repay the principal amount then due over a period of time instead of all at once.

The renewal agreement creates either a brand new mortgage or an extension of the original agreement. The lender is entitled, if it so desires, to rewrite the terms of the original contract. Not surprisingly, the most important of the terms is usually the new interest rate. A renewal agreement allows the lender to increase the interest rate if the old rate is lower than the current rates.

An obvious result of an increase in the mortgage rate is an increase in your monthly payments. Many people in the last few years, when the interest rates rose dramatically, were faced with almost a doubling of their interest rate and resulting mortgage payments. From its point of view, the lender is not increasing rates simply to gouge the public but to maintain the "spread" between its cost of money and the rate it lends at. Without this spread, lenders would not make a profit and we would quickly find sources of mortgage funds drying up!

Insurance is now available to borrowers to ensure that the interest rate on renewal will be fixed at a specific rate. For example, if you have a mortgage at 13%, and the interest rates climb to 18% when you want to renew, the mortgage insurance will ensure that your rate will not increase beyond a specified amount — say, 15% in this case.

There is an obvious advantage to a lender to renew a loan. The lender normally does not have to reappraise the property or review a new mortgage loan application. There is a certain amount of trust and confidence established between the two parties if payments have been made regularly over three or five years. The lender will, therefore, often be quite pleased to allow the payments to continue. However, if there have been some problems, the lender might take a more careful look at whether or not to give a renewal. Alternatively, a lender might allow a renewal but at an increased interest rate.

If the lender decides to offer you a renewal, it will usually forward the agreement to you about one month before the end of the term. The effect of your signing the renewal agreement will be to create a new mortgage contract. It may even be that the lender will not require a formal mortgage renewal agreement to be registered against the title to the property. Once agreed to, and signed, the renewal will bind both parties for the term of the renewal.

You do not have to accept the renewal proposal. You may not want to remain indebted to the lender. You are entitled to shop around for a new mortgage company or even negotiate with your existing lender in order to get the best rate. You should carefully examine the proposal for a renewal before accepting it. In this competitive day and age, many major lenders (particularly banks) allow and even encourage you to transfer your mortgage to them by offering this service at a very low cost. The advantages to you are that you don't have to prequalify and you become entitled to all benefits, such as prepayment options, that your new lender offers to its mortgage clients.

# b. PREPAYING YOUR MORTGAGE

The "payment" term of a mortgage is different from the "amortization" term. The payment term will generally run from 1 to 5 years while the amortization rate term can run up to 25 or 30 years. The amortization rate term is the length of time it would take, making the payments of principal and interest on a monthly basis, to pay off the mortgage in its entirety.

However, because most mortgage payment terms are far shorter than the amortization terms, when your payment term has expired there will be a substantial amount of principal still owing. In all likelihood, because mortgage payments are comprised of about 95% interest and 5% principal for the first couple of years, the mortgage principal balance will reduce very, very slightly. You are entitled to a statement from the lender stating exactly how much the principal balance of the mortgage is.

If you disagree with the numbers, it is quite a simple matter for you to order your own computer amortization table which will provide you with a monthly breakdown of how much principal and how much interest is paid in each mortgage payment.

In earlier times, when mortgage terms were 25 and 30 years, it was not until about the 20th year that large portions of the principal started to come off the mortgage. In these days of five-year terms or less, the principal balance reduces very, very slowly. Statistics have shown that if you pay a mortgage out over a period of 25 years, a $50 000 mortgage at an interest rate of 10% or 12% will cost you four or five times that amount. In order to reduce this high interest cost, especially because the dollars that you are paying on your mortgage payment are after-tax dollars and are not deductible, any opportunity that you get for prepayment under the mortgage should be taken advantage of.

Many mortgages are "closed mortgages." A closed mortgage means that you are not allowed to prepay any of the principal at any time during the term of the mortgage. Therefore, if your mortgage has a five-year term, the lender is not obligated to accept any payments from you except the monthly payments of principal and interest.

If the mortgage is an open mortgage, however, you are entitled to prepay at any time additional principal payments over and above the monthly payment. This is in your best interest because every dollar paid to principal will probably save four or five dollars' worth of interest in the long run.

Many lenders restrict this open privilege in any one of a number of ways. Some will allow a prepayment at any time but only in multiples of $100 and over.

Others, notably those that are part of the federal insurance program, only allow a prepayment of up to 10% of the principal balance and only on the anniversary date of the mortgage. This means that once per year, normally on the date when the first payment is made, you can pay up to 10% of the principal balance. This is an opportunity that you should take to reduce your long-term obligations.

Some mortgages currently offer better inducements by allowing borrowers the opportunity to pay more than 10% of the principal balance each year. As with most consumer purchases, it pays to shop around. Chapter 4 provides a discussion of new options currently being offered by mortgage lenders.

Unless the mortgage expressly says that it is an open mortgage, by allowing for some form of prepayment privilege, it cannot be paid off in full or in part without the consent of the lender. This confuses many people. They feel that if the mortgage says nothing about early prepayment, then the mortgage can automatically be paid off at any time. Unfortunately, this is not the case.

Basic contract law says that if parties have put their agreement in writing, then that written document will determine what the rights of each party are. If the contract is silent about prepayment, then the courts' attitude is that prepayment was not a part of the agreement.

Many mortgages allow you to pay off the mortgage upon payment to the lender of an additional three or six months' interest. This is in the mortgage document.

Under the Interest Act of Canada, any residential mortgage with a term that is longer than five years may be prepaid at any time after its fifth year whether or not the mortgage states this. Three months of interest must be paid to the lender. If the mortgage term is less than five years and is closed or locked in, no prepayment is allowed without the consent of the lender.

## c. PREPAYING A HIGH INTEREST MORTGAGE

If, for a variety of reasons, you presently find yourself with a high interest mortgage, there are some things you should be aware of if you are considering renewing or prepaying the mortgage.

Don't be fooled by a lender's offer to allow you to pay off the mortgage as long as you pay the "interest differential" plus a penalty. The interest differential is the total interest you would be paying until the mortgage term expires. What the lender is really saying is that if you prepay all interest that the lender is entitled to anyway calculated out over the balance of the mortgage term plus a penalty, you can pay the mortgage off. This is obviously not a good deal for you.

Here is a list of some things to examine if you have this renewal problem:

(a) Always check your mortgage; it may in fact allow prepayment with or without penalty.

(b) Contact your mortgage lender; some lenders may be prepared to lower your rate or allow a payout with only a minimal penalty.

(c) If you originally had a five-year mortgage, which you renewed, you may be entitled to pay your mortgage off with a three-month penalty; recent court cases in Ontario and B.C. support this, but legal assistance will likely be required to enforce your rights.

(d) If the lender verbally promised you that the rate could be renegotiated and you can prove this, you may have grounds to take legal action against the lender for damages. If you have a promise in writing so much the better.

(e) As lenders can be sensitive to public or government pressure, you may be successful if you make your problems public by writing to your M.P., provincial representative, local consumer group, newspaper or other media representatives. The more people who organize together in this way, the more effective you can be.

(f) If you deliberately refuse to make your mortgage payments, the lender may begin an action against you which would allow you to pay out the mortgage.

However, this is a risky business and will certainly not serve any useful purpose if you are attempting to arrange a new mortgage to pay off the existing one. Lenders simply do not look kindly upon this practice. It is effective only if you have come into substantial funds that you wish to use to retire the payments. Obtain some expert legal advice before embarking on this particular course.

(g) Some plans currently available from mortgage companies allow you to "double up" your monthly or weekly payments or pay an additional amount on your required payment. If possible, you should take advantage of these opportunities. Any extra payments you can make will be applied entirely against principal and will save you three or four times that amount in interest payments over the long run.

(h) Check with the municipal or provincial governments in your area; it is possible that some form of government subsidy or assistance program may still be in effect that you can take advantage of.

# 6

# DEFAULT UNDER A MORTGAGE

Like any other agreement entered into between two parties, the mortgage contract imposes obligations on both sides. The main obligation imposed on the lender is to lend the money on the security of the land. The lender, therefore, discharges this obligation early in the contractual arrangement by giving the money to the borrower.

However, the borrower's obligations continue. If the mortgage is for a five-year term, then the obligations of the borrower continue for that full five years. In fact, the main obligation of repaying the principal does not arise until the termination of the mortgage. However, throughout the term of the mortgage, the borrower has continuing obligations. If the borrower does not meet one or more of those obligations, it is deemed to be a "breach" or "default" under the mortgage. Once a breach or default occurs, the lender is entitled to use any one of a number of remedies that are allowed in the mortgage contract or by law.

This chapter discusses the types of breaches that can occur under a mortgage. The next chapter discusses some alternatives that you as a borrower have in these situations.

The mortgage contract contains many clauses, most of which are difficult to understand and almost never read by either the borrower or the borrower's advisors. The clauses impose a number of obligations on the borrower. Because the mortgage contract is in writing, and because it is signed by the borrower, the borrower is deemed to have full knowledge of all of the terms and conditions in the mortgage agreement. Therefore, it is not a defence in most cases to claim that you were not aware that a particular clause was in a mortgage simply because you did not read it.

There is really only one exception to this general rule of law. In situations where you can prove that the document

47

you signed was not the document that you thought you were to sign, or that the principal amount of the mortgage was different from the amount you thought you were securing your property on, the legal doctrine of *non est factum* may apply. This is a plea that you signed a contract with a mistaken impression of its content. This kind of matter will undoubtedly have to go to court.

What then are the types of default that can occur under a mortgage?

## a. FAILURE TO MAKE YOUR PAYMENTS

Non-payment of money due under the mortgage is the most serious (and common) default. Failure to make a mortgage payment on the day it is due is a breach of the mortgage contract. In the very early days of mortgages, this default resulted in the loss of the property. Things are not that harsh anymore.

If you make a payment that is due on the first of the month on the tenth of the month, the lender will not normally call in the mortgage unless the late payment is a continual problem. However, you will probably be responsible for late interest charges on payments not made on the due date.

There are no laws saying that a lender must wait one, two, three or six months after a breach before starting a legal action. Even a late payment that is quickly remedied is a breach. No matter how insignificant, a default has happened. If at sometime in the future, the matter ends up in court, the lender is entitled to provide evidence that payments have been habitually late. The court may consider this when setting a redemption period or providing some other form of relief to the lender.

In addition, if you fail to repay the principal amount due or renew the mortgage at the expiration of the mortgage term, it is a default under the mortgage. Most courts view this default as much more serious than the failure to make one or two mortgage payments during the term of the mortgage.

Interest payments under a mortgage often are much more complex and intricate than believed. There are very few mortgages that calculate interest payments strictly on the basis of the principal balance owing times the interest rate charged divided by the number of months in the year.

Most mortgages have interest rates that are "compounded" at least once or twice a year and often monthly. The effect of this is that any interest that is not paid when due can be added to the principal balance so that in future months, "new" interest will be calculated on the "old" interest. This is known as charging interest on interest or compounding the interest payments and is provided for in most standard mortgages.

Therefore, if mortgage payments are late or are not sufficient to cover principal and interest, lenders compound the outstanding payments. This rapidly builds up the balance owing on the mortgage. For people who are chronic late payers, the balance owing after one or two years of payments will actually be larger than the original principal balance.

In addition, all payments under a mortgage are applied first to the interest owing and then to the principal. Therefore, if not enough money has been paid to cover the outstanding interest or if payments are late, compounding will increase those amounts quite dramatically, especially in the first few years of the mortgage.

## b. FAILURE TO PAY YOUR TAXES

Most standard mortgages require you to pay all property taxes due on the mortgaged land. Some lenders require the borrower to make the payments to them and the lender then pays the property taxes as they come due. The lender is then assured that the taxes are paid on time. Not coincidentally, this also provides the lender with the free use of this money until the taxes have to be paid. Little, if any, interest is paid to the borrower, who derives no benefit from this arrangement.

A much better alternative is for you to pay your own taxes and keep the money in an interest bearing account until due. Many lenders, if requested, will allow you to do this as long as you have a good performance record with them.

Failure to either pay the taxes directly to the assessing authority or to pay the tax portion of the payments to the lender is a default under the mortgage. Continual failure to make these payments may result in the lender taking legal action on the basis that its security is seriously jeopardized.

Assessing authorities normally have the right by law to sell properties to provide funds for unpaid taxes. Naturally, a lender does not want to see land that it has lent money on sold at a public auction. It is quite likely that, if that occurred, the lender would not recover all of the principal owing.

You can, of course, remedy this default by paying the taxes due. However, this will not erase the fact that a default has occurred. It can be used in the future as evidence that you had a history of default. In most cases, if the taxes are paid in a reasonable time, a lender will not take any official action against you.

## c. FAILURE TO HAVE INSURANCE

For many purposes the lender may be thought of as an absentee landlord. For example, the lender has a vested interest in the land and any buildings on it and in fact, the buildings may be the most valuable part of the security. It is, therefore, very important to the lender that you keep adequate fire and other hazard insurance in force on the property.

The lender normally requires as part of the mortgage contract that the borrower maintain adequate insurance on the buildings. Failure to maintain adequate insurance will constitute a default under the mortgage. The lender can then claim damages from you on the basis that if, for example, a fire were to occur, there would not be sufficient funds available to replace the building and keep the lender's security in place.

If you forget or refuse to put insurance on the property, the lender has the choice of calling in the mortgage by taking some official step such as foreclosure or action for judicial sale. However, the lender will in all likelihood simply place its own insurance on the property and charge the cost of that insurance to you. Then, when you come to pay off the mortgage at the end of its term, you will have to pay for the insurance costs and will also be responsible for interest on that amount.

This is still classified as a breach, and the lender can use it as evidence in a future action.

## d. FAILURE TO KEEP PREMISES HABITABLE

Just as it is necessary to keep the property insured, it is necessary for you to keep the land and buildings in reasonable and habitable condition.

If a borrower allows the buildings (and to a certain extent the land as well) to run down, the value of the land and buildings will be diminished. This affects the security of the lender, especially if the lender holds a second or third mortgage on the property.

The question as to whether the property has been allowed to run down is much more difficult to determine than the question of non-payment. This will probably mean some sort of court action by the lender or perhaps the appointment of the lender to a position of mortgagee-in-possession (see chapter 7).

One way or another, the lender will undoubtedly take steps to improve the security by making whatever repairs or improvements are necessary. All of the costs of the repairs or improvements will be added to the mortgage balance and you will be responsible for repaying those costs plus interest.

Again, the lender may use this default as the reason for taking some official action to terminate the mortgage agreement.

# e. DAMAGING THE PROPERTY

Intentional "waste" or damage to the property is a breach. Unlike the situation where a borrower simply allows the property to deteriorate, this breach means the borrower has intentionally damaged the premises or done something harmful to the property. The lender is allowed to take steps to protect its position. One of those steps may be to have you removed from the premises.

The requirement not to intentionally damage the premises extends not only to the borrower but to the borrower's agents, employees, and tenants who are on the premises under a lease or licence agreement. Therefore, if you own rental property, and the tenant is intentionally causing damage, it is probably a default under the mortgage, and the lender can take some form of action on the mortgage.

Make sure that any tenants keep the premises in good condition. One way of providing for this protection is to put the requirement right in the lease contract.

# f. FAILURE TO OBEY THE LAW

You must comply with all the laws of the land. If you don't, it will be a breach under the mortgage. For example, if you own a duplex and use it as an illegal four-plex, it is a breach of a city by-law and will be a breach under the mortgage. Why? Because you broke a law, the legislating body (in this case the city council) has the power to impose sanctions against you which could either affect the lender's security or lower the value of the property.

# 7

# WHAT THE LENDER CAN DO
# IF YOU DEFAULT

Many people think that failure to make one mortgage payment will result in a visit to their home by the sheriff who will change the locks and throw them out into the streets. Nothing could be further from the truth.

Although the lender can take action that would result in the loss of your property, certain standard steps must be taken first.

The courts know that they are dealing with a very sensitive and, at times, emotional problem. They will bend over backwards to assist the homeowner.

Although we are primarily concerned with *your* rights when breaches occur, it is necessary to understand what the lender's rights are. Accordingly this chapter discusses the lender's rights in general and the next provides a province by province breakdown of specific variations.

Once any of the breaches discussed in chapter 6 occur, the lender is entitled to choose one of a number of remedies available. Most require the lender to use the courts, although there are exceptions to that rule.

## a. SEND A DEMAND LETTER

Most lenders who handle a large number of mortgages have an automatic system to handle defaults. After sending out a reminder letter or two, the lender will issue a demand letter. If it is ignored, the case will likely be turned over to the lender's lawyer for action. The lawyer may issue a demand letter or may begin legal action.

There is no real legal effect to the demand letter. The letter says that a payment has not been made or that some other breach under the mortgage has occurred. It then demands rectification of that breach within a set period of time. It states that if the matter is not remedied within a set period of time, the lender will begin some official form of legal action against you. Finally, the letter requires that along with rectification of the default, you make some additional payment to cover the costs of the demand letter.

The letter is sent by double registered mail. In most situations, the breach is non-payment of a mortgage payment that is due. The letter signifies that the lender is aware that the payment was not made and that you can no longer hope to rely on some foul-up in the lender's accounting system. Once a demand letter is received, you are on notice that if nothing is done some legal action is quite probable.

Although the use of the demand letter is an accepted practice, there is no requirement for the lender to send it. The basic reason the letter is sent is that a majority of breaches are rectified simply because the letter is sent out. It saves time and money for both parties and nips most problems in the bud.

Are you obliged to pay the additional costs set out in the demand letter? If you have missed some payments under your mortgage and receive a demand letter for the back payments, it may also say that you are required to pay an additional $50-$100 to cover the costs of sending the letter.

Although you may feel that this fee is a fairly hefty price to pay for a letter, you must check the mortgage itself to find out if this cost is valid. In most situations, the mortgage expressly states that in a default, the borrower is responsible for all of the legal costs incurred by the lender in taking action to remedy the problem.

If such a clause exists in the mortgage, then you are responsible for paying that amount. If you do not pay that amount, chances are that although the lender will accept the mortgage payments and discontinue further action against you, it will add the lawyer's charge to the principal balance of the mortgage. You will then be responsible for paying that amount back eventually and you will also pay interest on that amount.

Most provinces have a procedure known as "taxation" where legal costs can be reviewed by a court official and reduced if they are excessive.

## b. PAY YOUR TAXES FOR YOU

Standard mortgages contain a clause that allows the lender to make payments for such items as outstanding taxes, insurance, or money owing under previous mortgages. This clause ensures that the security of the land is kept in good standing. No lender wants to have the land upon which it has lent money in jeopardy because taxes have not been paid or insurance has not been placed on the premises.

The lender can rectify that breach by using its own funds to pay the debt. In order to recover this outlay of cash, the lender may simply add the cost to the principal balance of the mortgage and charge interest on the amount.

The lender does not have to take any other legal action against you. When the mortgage comes due, the lender will include in its final statement of money due, the additional amounts paid to cover those various costs. You are responsible for paying those amounts in addition to the principal balance left owing on the mortgage. This is a simple, effective remedy for the lender who is prepared to wait until the end of the mortgage term for repayment.

## c. ISSUE AN INJUNCTION

An injunction allows the lender to either prevent some illegal or improper activity from being carried out on the property or to require someone to do something that is necessary to keep the mortgage security in good standing.

For example, if you own revenue property and your tenants are damaging the property, the lender may obtain an injunction from the courts to keep the tenants off the premises and prevent further damage if you are unable or unwilling to do so. The costs associated with obtaining this injunction become your responsibility.

## d. SELL YOUR GOODS

Another clause normally found in a mortgage is the "attornment" clause. This clause provides that the borrower, for certain purposes, is deemed to become the tenant of the lender. The lender becomes a landlord with rent payable by the "tenant" to the "landlord" in an amount equivalent to the mortgage payments due.

You may think that this is a very unusual type of clause to find in a mortgage. However, the reason is simple enough. In a typical landlord and tenant situation, one of the rights of a landlord when the rent has not been paid is to "distrain" for rent. This means that the landlord, when rent is in arrears, can instruct the sheriff, a judicial official, to seize goods owned by the tenant from the tenant's possession. If the tenant does not pay the rent due, those goods are sold to cover the amount of the arrears.

By including an attornment clause in a mortgage, the lender hopes to use this technique if mortgage payments are not paid.

This procedure is strictly controlled by statute in every province. The restrictions on it are normally severe enough to discourage most lenders from doing this. They cannot sell the goods of anyone except the actual borrower and even these goods cannot be seized if they are "exempt" from seizure. The type and value of the exempted goods vary from province to province.

## e. TAKE POSSESSION

Most standard mortgages provide that in a default, the lender is entitled to take possession of the premises to preserve its security. This is called mortgagee in possession.

This right to possession, depending on the province, may be exercised independently or as part of a combined action. The lender does not have to obtain a special court order, although, if required, it can be obtained very quickly.

To take possession of the premises, the lender must give proper notice to the borrower; an attornment clause in the mortgage is not sufficient.

A second mortgagee may take possession but at all times will be operating subject to the rights of the first mortgagee.

While in possession, the lender is entitled to all rents and profits generated from the land and is also entitled to be reimbursed for expenses incurred. The lender is required to maintain the premises in a reasonable state of repair and is liable for deterioration or waste.

In addition, the lender may also have to pay rent to the borrower. An accounting by the lender to the borrower is required to ensure that money collected by the lender does not exceed the amount due under the mortgage.

The lender that takes possession must scrupulously administer the premises in order to avoid problems. This is one of the few rights of a lender that can, in fact, put it at risk. It is not often used except in serious situations involving revenue properties that are not being administered by the borrower. It is rarely used for residential homes.

A mortgagee in possession cannot voluntarily abandon possession; a court order or the consent of the borrower is required to terminate the possession.

## f. PUT THE PROPERTY INTO RECEIVERSHIP

If a lender does not wish to take on the potential liabilities and responsibilities of a mortgagee in possession, it has the right to apply for the appointment of an independent party known as a receiver or receiver-manager to take possession of the property to preserve it pending litigation.

Like the mortgagee in possession, a receiver can be appointed either through the courts or privately. A receiver can be appointed privately only if the mortgage allows such an appointment. In most situations, an application is made for a court appointed receiver. This provides protection for the lender because the receiver will be sanctioned by the court and the borrower or any tenants on the property will have no recourse against the receiver.

The main purpose of the receivership is to preserve and protect the property pending the litigation. However, the receiver has basically the same rights that a mortgagee in possession has.

As with a mortgagee in possession, a receiver may be appointed *ex parte* (without notice) where an emergency situation exists. The receiver is also required to keep accurate records and to have the accounts approved by the court when the receivership has been completed.

## g. SUE FOR THE BORROWER'S PERSONAL FUNDS

Although the land is put up as security, the borrower's prime responsibility is to repay the loan. This is called the borrower's "personal covenant."

If the payments are not made, the lender has the right to bring a lawsuit against the borrower claiming the money from the borrower's personal funds. Once the money is paid, the land that forms the security is released by the lender.

This remedy is usually used by the lender in conjunction with other remedies discussed later. It is particularly useful when a lender realizes that if the land is sold, there would be insufficient funds generated from that sale to pay off the mortgage debt. Therefore, this action is often joined with a foreclosure or sale action in order that any "shortfall" (the difference between the amount of money from the sale and the total amount owing) would be owed by the borrower to the lender.

Naturally, if a shortfall is anticipated and an action on the personal covenant is not taken, the lender will not be able to collect the shortfall.

The liability of the borrower under the personal covenant actually remains in effect even though the property may have been sold.

When two borrowers sign a mortgage jointly, they are jointly and individually liable to pay the lender. This means that the lender has the right to sue for the personal funds of either or both of the mortgagors for the full amount. Only if the lender releases the borrower from the personal obligation will the liability cease.

A purchaser who assumes the mortgage, even though that person may not have actually contracted with the lender, becomes liable on the personal covenant once in possession of the premises. The liability remains in effect while that person is in possession. If that purchaser sells the property to other purchasers who assume the mortgage, the liability transfers to the new party in possession, although the transferor may remain liable for arrears at the time of transfer.

If the mortgage is a collateral mortgage, then the situation is different. A collateral mortgage provides some other form of security. In most cases this security is a promissory note or, on occasion, a personal guarantee. Therefore, there is always personal liability in these mortgages. If the loan goes into default, the lender will take action on the mortgage and can also act against the borrower personally. The personal action may be the primary action and the mortgage brought into it simply because the mortgage is part of the security.

If any of your other assets form part of a mortgage security, then those assets are at risk. For example, a bank may make a loan to your business in return for a mortgage on your house and a chattel mortgage on your vehicle. In a default, not only does the bank have the right to begin action but also to have the car sold and the proceeds applied to reduce the debt. However, only those assets that are specifically part of the security are at risk.

The only way that all of your assets may be at risk is if the lender is able to successfully sue you on the personal covenant that you have given under the mortgage.

However, some provinces, such as Alberta, have legislation that relieves individual borrowers from being personally liable under a mortgage. This means that the lender is unable to sue the borrower personally and must proceed only against the secured land. In those provinces, the lender may not sue you even if the property is sold and the funds do not cover the mortgage debt. (See chapter 8.)

## h. ACCELERATE THE MORTGAGE

Another clause that is often found in mortgages is known as the "acceleration" clause. It allows the lender to "accelerate" the payments due once a breach has occurred.

The effect of this is that even though a mortgage may have three or four years left on its term, a lender is entitled to claim the full amount of the principal balance plus all interest due if you default.

Therefore, subject to action by the courts, you are required to come up with the full amount owing even though you may only have been in default for one or two mortgage payments.

The use of the acceleration clause in an action on the personal covenant allows the lender to claim the full amount owing under the mortgage rather than just what the arrears are at that time.

## i. SELL YOUR PROPERTY

The lender has the right to exercise the "power of sale," which means that your property can be advertised and sold if you do not remedy a breach after having received notice of that breach.

For example, in Ontario a standard mortgage provides that the lender has the right to sell the premises 35 days after notice of default has been given to the borrower.

The 35-day period allows the borrower to remedy the defect. If the defect is remedied, then the rights of sale cease and the mortgage again is in good standing.

If the defect is not remedied within the notice period, the lender is free to immediately sell the property. No court order or other legal action is necessary, and the third party purchaser who acquires the property from the lender will get good title.

Any excess money received by the lender on the sale must be paid to the borrower. In addition, the lender has a legal and ethical duty to ensure that the price it advertises and gets for the property is bona fide. In order to do this, the lender will obtain appraisals for the property and advertise it extensively.

The courts will examine any sale very closely to ensure that the lender is not selling the property to itself or to another person in trust for itself.

A lender who has given the notice of sale cannot begin any other action on the mortgage such as foreclosure or an action for possession. Power of sale proceedings will later enable the lender to enforce the security as well as sue for personal funds if the money received from the sale does not cover the mortgage.

Because the power of sale allows the lender to act independently, the courts carefully control the procedure involved in giving notice as well as the attempts to sell and the terms of the ultimate sale.

Although the power of sale is a quick remedy, it cannot be combined with any other remedies available under the mortgage. It must be done before or after any of the other major remedies are tried. For example, if the lender begins proceedings that entitle the borrower to defend or redeem, the lender is generally not entitled to serve a notice of sale until the court proceedings have been completed or until the borrower's rights in those proceedings have expired.

## j. FORECLOSURE

Most people use the term "foreclosure" to apply to any action taken by a lender. In fact, foreclosure is a specific remedy different from all the others discussed.

It is a popular remedy in the land titles jurisdiction provinces of Alberta and Saskatchewan but, because of the availability of other remedies such as the power of sale, it is not used as frequently in Ontario.

Foreclosure is available to a lender if you fail to pay the principal and interest due under the mortgage. However, in some cases, foreclosure action may be taken for not paying taxes or money due under the mortgage agreement.

Foreclosure begins when the lender asks the court to extinguish the borrower's equity or redemption rights in the land and transfer all legal interest, including the right to possession and legal title, to the lender.

In a foreclosure action, the lender asks the court to "foreclose" you out of your right of redemption. Any equity you may have built up in the property is then passed on to the lender and you receive nothing from any subsequent sale. The lender is entitled to all of the profits.

There can be no foreclosure without a judicial order, so the procedure involves a legal process. The courts must exercise an equitable discretion on behalf of a borrower. This means that if you provide the court with evidence of your intent to pay, the court will in many cases give you time to pay up the arrears. This extra period of time is known as the "redemption period."

It is determined by the courts on a case by case basis. Many factors are considered — some legal and some non-legal. They include your equity position, whether the mortgage has expired, the existence of second or third mortgages, market conditions, and the number and age of your children.

Based on those factors, a court will set a specific time in which you can either pay off the mortgage in full or pay all arrears and costs. Depending on the situation, the redemption period can range from one day to one year.

You are normally entitled to exclusive possession of the premises during the entire redemption period.

Foreclosure may be combined with a number of other remedies. In many jurisdictions, it is combined with the right of judicial sale (see below). This allows the lender to sell the property in a judicial sale, but if it does not sell, the title to the property can be transferred to the lender.

A foreclosure action can also be combined with an action on the personal covenant in case the proceeds of a sale do not cover the amount due. Often, it is combined with an application to appoint a receiver or to have a lender take possession of the property.

If a foreclosure action is started by a first mortgagee and there is a second mortgage as well, all of the rights of the second mortgagee against the land are wiped out unless the second mortgagee takes steps to "redeem" the amount due under the first mortgage. (See chapter 12.)

## k. HAVE A JUDICIAL SALE

A judicial sale is generally combined with other remedies, usually an action for foreclosure.

A judicial sale is supervised by the courts. The sale is done by tender or by public auction. It may also be done by private agreement between the lender and a third party as long as the agreement is ratified by the courts.

In all situations, the court supervises the sale to ensure that it is an arm's length sale and that all the proper notices are given to all parties involved. This includes notices to you and to second or third mortgagees.

This is a unique remedy because the borrower has the right to request this sale. This is discussed in more detail later.

Lenders use a judicial sale action when they believe they will be able to be paid out of the sale proceeds. They also use a judicial sale when the borrower has no money and a personal judgment against the borrower would be of no benefit.

## l. SUE PREVIOUS OWNERS

In certain situations, if you own a home and sell it to a purchaser who assumes your mortgage, you could be faced with an unpleasant situation. If your purchaser, or even a purchaser of *your* purchaser, defaults on the mortgage, the lender may be able to sue not only the existing house owner, but may also have the right to sue all previous borrowers under the mortgage, including you, especially if the lender did not approve the transfer or assumption of the mortgage when you sold the house.

Laws vary in each province regarding this right. In those provinces where approval of the mortgage lender is required before the mortgage is assumed, you should obtain a written release of any future claims against you from the lender.

Another alternative is to obtain a written indemnity from your purchaser. An indemnity is a promise by the purchaser to repay any monies you have to pay to the mortgage company regarding future default on the mortgage by any party.

When you sell your house, it is wise to obtain legal advice so that if potential liability under a mortgage exists you can protect yourself.

# 8
## PROVINCIAL VARIATONS IN PROCEDURE

This chapter discusses the procedures involved in a mortgage action on a province by province basis. This is a very technical area of law, especially in provinces like Ontario where a number of remedies are available. This will be a summary only, and will give a sample of the variety of laws. If you need more information, or if you live in a province or territory not covered in this chapter, you should seek advice from your lawyer.

In all cases, there are specific technical rules that must be followed. For example, in order to inform you of the action or any application to the court, the lender must serve you with copies of all the necessary papers. You usually must be served personally with the documents, especially when the action is begun.

By avoiding personal service, you can, of course, buy some time. However, it will not benefit you forever. Sooner or later, the lender will be able to obtain a court order eliminating the need for personal service. Then the documents will be served "substitutionally" as the court directs. This might mean leaving the documents at your house or with some adult person living with you or advertising the notice in a local newspaper.

The danger to you is that, if served substitutionally, you may not even know an action has been started or is continuing. The advantage gained initially may ultimately become a large disadvantage. It is imperative that you be aware of the status of the mortgage action.

## a. BRITISH COLUMBIA
Some of the statutes in British Columbia that deal with mortgages are:

(a) The Law and Equity Act

(b) The Land Title Act

(c) The Condominium Act

Under British Columbia law, an action is begun with a "petition." The action generally is against both the individual borrower and the land. Recent changes to the law require that the legal action be commenced in the registry where the land is located. This means that in British Columbia you can be sued on your personal covenant under the mortgage.

If you do not respond to the petition with an "appearance notice," the mortgagee is entitled to an order "nisi." The order nisi from the court sets a redemption period. During this redemption period, you have the right to either bring the mortgage back into good standing by paying the amount of the arrears plus costs or paying off the mortgage.

Although the normal redemption period is six months from the date of the order nisi, the court has the discretion to reduce this redemption period.

At the expiration of the redemption period, if the property is still in default, the lender is then entitled to either take title to the property or sell the property and get a deficiency judgment for any shortfall.

The process by which the lender takes title is known as foreclosing out the interest held by the borrower. When the lender takes title, you lose any rights you had in the property and the lender is entitled to ownership and possession of the premises.

Instead of taking title, the lender may apply for an order for sale which will allow it to sell the property. If there is a deficiency after the sale, the lender can then sue you on your personal covenant. The sale is always subject to court supervision. It normally takes place by sealed tenders.

If the final order for foreclosure is granted, and the lender decides to take the property rather than sell it, the lender is not able to later proceed against you on your personal covenant.

Lenders also have the right to obtain an order appointing a receiver or allowing the lender to take possession of the property as a mortgagee in possession.

Notice of the steps involved in the action is required to be given to most "interested" parties. These include all other parties that have something registered against the property and, of course, the borrower. That, coupled with the redemption period, means that the entire action could take up to one full year even if you do nothing.

If you want to become involved in the action, you should start when the redemption period is determined. At this hearing, you can give your evidence about the value of the property and any special factors that might be relevant and ask the court to grant the longest redemption period possible. The court has the power to shorten a redemption period and if there is very little equity involved it may well do so.

During the redemption period, the lender can accept payments and must give credit to the borrower for all of those payments.

You have the right to redeem the mortgage at any time up to the final order for foreclosure. There are even some cases that suggest a borrower may have the right to redeem the mortgage even after a court ordered sale has been approved. Legal advice is recommended if you are in that position.

You may apply to the courts at any time during the action to ask for an extension of the redemption period. For example, if the redemption period has expired and you are in the middle of arranging new financing, the court may grant an extension or you may apply to have some input in the marketing or the sale as ordered by the courts.

In addition, applications to court may be appealed to higher levels of the judiciary under certain circumstances. However, to be successful, you will have to prove that some legal principle was wrongly interpreted at the original hearing.

Once the final order for foreclosure has been granted and the appeal period has expired or an order for sale has been made and approved by the courts, your rights are extinguished.

## b. ALBERTA

In Alberta, an action on a mortgage is called a foreclosure action. The action is begun in a statement of claim. It is a claim by the lender for a number of remedies including an action on the borrower's personal covenant.

The relevant statutes involved in a foreclosure action in Alberta include:

(a) The Land Titles Act, which establishes the registration system for mortgages in Alberta and the rights of the parties in terms of priorities

(b) The Law of Property Act, which provides the courts with the equitable jurisdiction they need to provide relief to borrowers in certain circumstances

Once you have been properly served with the documents, the lender will apply to the courts for an "order nisi/order for sale." During this application, the court will set a redemption period. During the redemption period, you may either pay off the mortgage or pay up all of the arrears plus costs.

If you are unable to do either of those two things, at the end of the nisi perod, notice of a judicial sale will be given to all interested parties involved in the mortgage. Once that notice has been given (and in some cases, this notice can be done away with), the property will be advertised for sale in a local newspaper. The sale is by sealed tender (offer). No "minimum" tender price or other monetary information is included in the advertisement. Tenders for the purchase of that property are then open for acceptance.

If no tenders are received, the court may order that the property be readvertised, or it can grant a final order for foreclosure, which vests legal title to the property in the name of the lender.

If tenders are received, the court will assess the prices and then make an order accepting or rejecting any one of them. If a tender is accepted, a court order will be granted stating that upon payment by the tenderer of the balance of the tender funds into court (a 10% deposit is required), the title will be vested in the name of the tenderer free and clear of any encumbrances except those stated in the court order. At that time, your interest will be extinguished, and the court will order that the tenderer be entitled to possession of the subject property.

If the tender is rejected by the courts, the property may be readvertised or vested in the name of the lender.

If the property is sold in a judicial sale, the borrower (if an individual) is granted relief from forfeiture. This means that there can be no personal claim against the borrower for any deficiency. In effect, therefore, the owner of residential premises has no personal liability to the lender.

This may not be the case in situations involving commercial or investment property or property in the name of a corporation, but an individual homeowner in Alberta need not usually fear being subject to any personal liability, although recent cases suggest that if you assume a mortgage originally granted to a corporation, the lender may be able to claim against you personally. In addition, borrowers with mortgages insured by CMHC or granted by CMHC and the Alberta Home Mortgage Corporation may, because of recent decisions, be personally liable for deficiencies.

You may intervene in the action at any time. If you do not have a valid defence to the action, you may file a "demand of notice" form, which entitles you to full notice of the action. You are, therefore, entitled to give evidence to the court about the redemption period. In Alberta, assuming there is some equity in the property, the redemption period on urban land is generally six months and on rural land, one year. In a typical situation, a foreclosure on a residence takes at least one year for urban property and even longer for rural homestead lands.

You are entitled to redeem the mortgage at any time prior to the final order that vests title in the lender's name or approves a sale to a tenderer. You can either pay the arrears plus the costs or pay off the mortgage entirely.

In Alberta, the lender has many of the same remedies that are available in most jurisdictions, including the right to have a receiver appointed, to obtain an injunction or obtain the rights of a mortgagee in possession. The "power of sale" remedy is not available.

The intervention of a borrower in an Alberta action will normally be confined to applying for the longest redemption period possible. In addition, the borrower may wish to ask for a readvertising of the property if either low tenders or no tenders are received.

A recent decision from the Alberta courts suggests that the relief against personal liability of individuals to the lender also extends to collateral mortgages as well as conventional mortgages.

## c. SASKATCHEWAN

The relevant statutes involved in actions in Saskatchewan are:

(a) Land Contracts (Actions) Act

(b) Homeowners Protection Act

(c) Land Titles Act

Under the Land Contracts (Actions) Act, no action for the sale or possession of land can be begun without the approval of the court.

If the court consents, the lender is entitled to begin an action with a statement of claim. In the statement of claim, the lender asks for an order nisi and foreclosure of the property or a judicial sale.

If you do not defend the action or ask for a judicial sale, the property will end up with the lender on expiration of the redemption period. A judicial sale will be by public auction rather than by closed tender. If a bid is received at the auction that will pay the lender as well as all of the costs involved, that bidder will obtain the property. Otherwise, the property will end up in the name of the lender and your rights will be extinguished.

In a Saskatchewan action, you have the choice of appearing before the court and requesting a judicial sale of the property. If you do not, you lose all rights (and any equity) in the property upon expiration of the redemption period.

Under the Limitations of Civil Rights Act, the lender's rights are restricted to the land mortgage; you cannot personally be sued for payment on a residential mortgage.

## d. MANITOBA

The relevant legislation in Manitoba includes:

(a) The Law of Property Act

(b) The Mortgage Act

(c) The Real Property Act

In Manitoba, once a mortgage is one month in arrears a lender is entitled to start proceedings by filing a notice exercising power of sale. This notice is served on all parties who appear on the title.

If the arrears are not brought up to date within 30 days, the lender is entitled to apply to the court for an order for sale. At this point, the lender will go to court to obtain mortgage sale conditions. Once approved, a sale of the mortgaged property will be ordered. The sale will be by public auction.

If a bid is not received equal to the amount of a reserve bid, the sale will be deemed to be abortive. The reserve bid is the amount of the mortgage principal plus the total of all prior mortgages and costs. Because the reserve bid is not disclosed, anyone bidding on the property must gamble on the amount to bid.

If a bid is made in excess of or equal to the reserve bid, the property will be sold to the bidder. Any excess money will go to subsequent encumbrancers and ultimately to you.

If there is a shortfall, you may be personally liable. There is no legislation in Manitoba providing relief from personal liability.

If no bid is received, the lender must apply to the court for an order for foreclosure. If a final order for foreclosure is granted, title to the mortgaged property will end up in the name of the lender, and any rights you have will be foreclosed out.

Although there is no set redemption period, the procedure for obtaining the final order for foreclosure usually takes six months from the time of the original notice. You have the right to redeem the mortgage at any time before the final order is granted.

In addition, you have the right to apply to the court for adjournments during the application for the final foreclosure or ask for an adjournment of the auction. The court has discretion to grant those types of delays depending on the circumstances.

### e. ONTARIO

The relevant statutes in Ontario include:

(a) The Land Titles Act

(b) The Mortgages Act

(c) The Registry Act

(d) The Short Form of Mortgages Act

All of the remedies discussed earlier (e.g., the right to distrain for rent, receivership, injunction) are available to Ontario lenders. However, the power of sale remedy is the most popular. The foreclosure remedy ranks a distant second.

The advantage of the power of sale remedy is that it can take place quickly and is less costly than other remedies. The major disadvantage is that the lender must account for the proceeds of the sale and in many cases will have to sue separately for possession.

Fifteen days after a default has occurred, a lender is entitled to serve a notice of sale on the borrower and all subsequent encumbrancers. This begins the power of sale procedure. In the notice, you are given 35 days to pay off all arrears and costs. Because the notice must be served on all subsequent encumbrancers, they also have the right to pay the arrears.

If no one clears up the arrears, the lender is entitled to sell the property either in a private or public sale. Most commonly, the property is listed for sale with a real estate company.

It is only necessary to put the mortgage into good standing — the full amount of the mortgage need not be paid out. During this 35-day period, the lender can take no further action on the property. However, if the property is not redeemed by the expiration of the time period, the lender is entitled to conduct a sale.

The lender has a duty to obtain a fair and reasonable price for the property, and this price may be reviewed by the court. In fact, the court scrutinizes the sale very closely to ensure that the sale was bona fide and at arm's length.

The lender is entitled to sue for any deficiency once the property has been sold. However, once the notice of sale is given, no proceedings of any sort may be taken by the lender to enforce the security or the debt until the time specified in the notice has elapsed. However, you may ultimately be personally liable for any shortfall that exists as long as the sale price was reasonable and acceptable to the courts.

This is important because under power of sale, a lender is not entitled to possession of the property. If the lender requires possession of the property, it will have to be obtained prior to giving the notice of sale or after the notice period has expired. Additionally, a lender cannot begin a foreclosure action until the notice of sale period has expired.

You must be prepared to act quickly if you receive a notice of sale. The obvious thing to do is to pay up the arrears. If this is impossible, contact the lender directly to discuss alternatives.

The second most common procedure available to a lender in Ontario is foreclosure. This is an application by the lender to foreclose or negate the borrower's interest in the property and to remove the borrower's right to redeem it.

A foreclosure action is started with a writ of summons. The lender normally requests foreclosure, personal action on the covenant, and possession of the property. This writ is served on all parties, including subsequent encumbrancers who are made parties to the action.

Once served, you or any of the defendants, may file a notice desiring an opportunity to redeem (a notice DOR). This automatically results in a stay of the proceedings and is in effect a redemption period. Six to nine months is the usual time allowed for redemption. If the property is not redeemed within that time, the lender will be in a position to obtain a final order of foreclosure. The lender may then keep the property, sell it or rent it. Any equity that you have reverts to the lender who may ultimately profit from holding the land.

Instead of filing a notice DOR, you may file a notice desiring sale. A judgment may then be signed by the court granting an immediate sale of the property. This sale will be supervised by the courts like a judicial sale.

If you do not file either the notice DOR or the notice desiring sale, then the lender may apply for a judgment for immediate foreclosure of the property, for possession, and for payment on your personal covenant.

You might not want to request the judicial sale if there appears to be substantial equity in the property. The prices obtained in these sales are normally below market value. Ironically, a judicial sale may also be harmful if you have no equity in the property. If there is a deficiency on the sale, you are personally liable for that amount.

If the lender has begun action, you merely have to pay the amount of money owing plus the costs as provided for under the Ontario Mortgage Act.

Similarly, if a demand has been made but no action begun, you merely have to pay the arrears and the costs rather than the full amount of the mortgage.

In Ontario, an action on the personal covenant for payment exists as an independent remedy although the action may be combined with foreclosure or a power of sale proceeding. You may have personal liability even if the lender forecloses out your interest.

The courts in Ontario have adopted a liberal approach regarding the ability of borrowers to redeem the property even in power of sale situations. However, once a sale has been made, in order to preserve the property, you must pay off the entire mortgage plus all costs of the foreclosure. Prior to the sale, it is possible to redeem the mortgage simply by paying the arrears and the costs.

## f. QUEBEC

Legislation dealing with mortgages in Quebec is derived from the Napoleonic Code and is different in many ways from the laws in other provinces. We speak of *mortgaging* property in the rest of Canada, but in Quebec, it is a *hypothecation*. Quebec also has counterparts to other terms and procedures common to the rest of the country.

In effect, there is no actual foreclosure procedure in Quebec as the initial transaction is not a mortgage transaction. The lending of money on the security of real estate is supported by a "deed of loan with hypothec." In the deed the borrower acknowledges the loan and promises to repay it. You can be sued for non-performance, and if the lender's action is successful, judgment is granted and the lender may proceed to collect from your assets.

In a purely hypothecary action, the lender is directed toward debt realization by a forced judicial sale of the property. The actions of property sale and collection of monies from the debtor may be separate but the usual practice is to combine them. The Quebec civil code contains the procedural provisions for these actions. While the underlying legal principles in Quebec may be different from those in other provinces, the result is the same. A lender is entitled to seek a sheriff's sale of the land and can bid on it along with any third party.

When the lender receives judgment for its claim and acquires the property for a bid that is less than the total claim, the lender is entitled to enforce collection of the balance from your other assets. However, amendments to the civil code include provisions for you to obtain your release when the property acquired by the lender has a value of at least the total amount of the lender's claim and any other claims that rank ahead of the hypothecary. If the lender has sold the property for a price at least equal to its claim, including expenses plus interest, you may also obtain your release.

Unlike the laws in other provinces, an action taken by a second mortgage lender on property may have a definite effect on the first mortgage lender. The usual case is that the position and security of the first mortgage holder would be undisturbed by an action commenced by the second mortgage holder. In Quebec, however, the action by the second mortgage holder can result in a forced sale of the property. When such a sale takes place the first mortgagee must either bid at the sale or take its chances on receiving enough from the sale proceeds to repay the loan.

Because of the community property concept in Quebec, the law may also differ on the obligation of spouses to sign hypothecs. Legal advice should be obtained to determine the obligations and rights of spouses in each case.

## g. NEW BRUNSWICK
The relevant legislation regulating mortgages in New Brunswick includes —
   (a) The Property Act
   (b) The Registry Act
   (c) The Land Titles Act
   (d) The Standard Forms of Conveyances Act
   (e) The Sale of Lands Publication Act

The main remedy available to a lender under the laws of New Brunswick is the power of sale. Once the mortgage goes into default, the lender has the right to serve notice on you. If the mortgage arrears are not paid, the property can be sold by private or public auction. The lender must give you four weeks' notice and prior notice of the proposed sale must be published in a newspaper.

The lender has the right to bid on the property. There is no "reserved bid" system in effect which would require that proposed bidders meet a minimum value standard. However, the property cannot be sold for a price substantially below its appraised value.

Lenders also have the right of foreclosure. As well, you are liable on your personal covenant to the lender for any amount still owing after the property has been sold.

## h. NOVA SCOTIA

The statute in Nova Scotia dealing with mortgages is the Judicature Act.

Foreclosure is the most common form of relief used by lenders in this province. Notice of the foreclosure proceedings must be given to you. If you do not respond to the notice, the lender must appear in court and, upon proof of the service of notice and the amount owing, the court can order that the property be sold and the proceeds paid to the lender. If there is still an amount owing after the proceeds are paid to the lender, you are liable for the difference.

The Nova Scotia Judicature Act contains an interesting provision. It allows you to ask the court to discontinue a foreclosure action if you pay all arrears owing and any costs that have been incurred by the lender to the date of the court application. However, you are entitled to do this only once on the same mortgage. If you default a second time under the same mortgage, the assistance of the court is not available to prevent a foreclosure action from being completed. At that point, it would be the lender's decision whether or not to discontinue the legal action.

If the property does go through the foreclosure process, the sheriff advertises and conducts the sale. The method of sale is strictly up to the discretion of the court. Accordingly, sales can be held by public or private auction, sheriff's sale or tender.

# i. PRINCE EDWARD ISLAND

Legislation in Prince Edward Island dealing with mortgages and foreclosures includes the following:

   (a)  The Registry Act

   (b)  The Real Property Act

   (c)  The Family Law Reform Act

Laws affecting mortgages in Prince Edward Island are similar to the laws of the other Maritime Provinces. Mortgage lenders normally rely on the power of sale remedy to recover monies in a default on a residential mortgage. Other remedies available include the right of foreclosure and an action on the personal covenant against the borrower.

As in other provinces, the courts have the power to exercise a broad discretion which allows them to treat a homeowner in a fair and equitable way while at the same time making sure that the lender's rights are adequately protected.

Because of unusual laws in Prince Edward Island dealing with ownership of land, legal advice is recommended for both the potential borrower and the lender.


# j. NEWFOUNDLAND

The relevant statutes which regulate mortgages in Newfoundland are the following:

   (a)  The Conveyancing Act

   (b)  The Judicature Act

The main right available to a lender in Newfoundland is the power of sale. The lender is afforded broad rights under the appropriate legislation to serve notice of default on a borrower and sell the subject property if the arrears owing are not brought up to date.

Before exercising the sale right however, the lender must serve at least one month's notice on you. After one month, the lender is free to take steps to sell the property.

In addition to the power of sale remedy, a lender also has the right of foreclosure. The court is also given wide discretion to grant orders for sale or redemption of property depending on each situation's circumstances.

Newfoundland also has instituted certain laws requiring foreign mortgage holders to have registered "attorneys" in the province. Legal advice should be sought by lenders wishing to make mortgage loans in this province.

# 9

# WHAT YOU CAN DO IF YOU FALL BEHIND IN PAYMENTS

The obvious solution to any default is to rectify it. If the default involves falling behind in payments, it can be rectified by paying the money due. The lender is not always obligated to accept the money, but in most jurisdictions and in most circumstances, a lender will accept a late payment because it is cheaper in the long run to take the payment rather than allow the mortgage to go into default.

You will be charged interest for late payments but this is certainly much cheaper for you than a full foreclosure or other action. The late interest charge will usually be at the same rate as the mortgage interest.

If the default does not involve the payments to the lender, then the remedy is to comply with the requirements of the mortgage. This might mean getting insurance or repairing damage to the property. Find out exactly what is required (assuming that the demands are reasonable).

Once the default has been corrected, you are entitled to receive confirmation that the mortgage is in good standing. Request a confirming letter from the lender. Although the lender is not obliged to provide you with this letter, the fact that you have sent a letter and that it has not been questioned by the lender may be useful to you if the mortgage goes into default in the future.

The remaining suggestions in this chapter deal with the non-payment of mortgage payments. This default probably covers more than 90% of those that occur each year.

First, put yourself in the lender's position to assess both the strengths and weaknesses of the lender's position.

Most mortgage loans are made by companies in the business of lending money; you are dealing with banks, trust companies, co-ops or other institutions. They rely on profit, which is the "spread" between what they pay to borrow money and what they collect to lend it. Included in their analysis of profits is the cost of administration of the mortgage and, to a certain extent, the charges associated with late payments, etc. However, lenders are very reluctant to allow mortgages to go into default. They count on having the use of that money coming in to re-use and increase profits.

Therefore, in most circumstances the lender will want to work out some type of deal with you. However, it may be more difficult to make a deal with a lender that holds an insured mortgage.

Because a lender is in the business of lending money, the last thing that it wants is to end up owning land. The lender is not equipped to hold or sell real estate nor does it want to.

The lender is primarily interested in the return of its money plus interest. In days of decreasing property values and economic slowdown, lenders are even more motivated to do what they can to obtain repayment of the funds.

Based on the above, here are some suggestions to consider in dealing with your mortgage company.


## a. RESCHEDULE THE DEBT

There are many alternatives available to a borrower in dealing with mortgage arrears. Although there is a contract, it is certainly quite possible with the consent of both parties to re-arrange the mortgage payments in some way that would benefit both parties. It certainly benefits the lender by ensuring that at least some of the money is paid and it benefits you because the mortgage would not go into default.

Some of the ways of rescheduling the mortgage debt are as follows.

## 1. Capitalize the amount owing

"Capitalizing" the amount owing involves determining how much unpaid interest is due and adding that amount to the outstanding principal loan on the mortgage. For example, if the principal balance of your mortgage is $50 000 and you have been unable to meet your monthly payments of $500 for the last six months, you can add the $3 000 of outstanding interest onto the $50 000 principal balance so that the mortgage principal becomes $53 000. The effect of this is that you will be paying interest on $53 000 rather than $50 000.

Eventually the lender will receive the full amount due plus the bonus of getting interest on the outstanding interest. For you, of course, it will mean that the arrears will be wiped out and you will be able to start out fresh. But because the principal balance has increased, the monthly payments will also go up slightly.

## 2. Change the interest rate

Many mortgages that are on a floating rate or that were taken out in 1980, 1981 or early 1982 carried a high interest rate. Sometimes the high monthly payments that result simply cannot be made.

It is possible on occasion to negotiate a reduction of the interest rate to a more manageable level for a year or two of the term with the interest rate increasing toward the end of the term. For example, if your mortgage is an 18% mortgage with a three-year term, you could reduce the payments for the next 12 months to 15%, increase the payments to 15-1/2% in the second year, and up to 23-1/2% in the third year. The lender over the three years would still average a return of 18% but you would have a couple of years at a lower rate. By the time the third year rolled around, you would have a higher income to cover the higher payments or might be able to re-negotiate or refinance the entire mortgage at the current rates, if lower.

### 3. Pay graduated mortgage payments

Graduated mortgage payments combine the two previous suggestions; basically, you would keep your total mortgage payments as low as possible for the first year or two of the term and allow the mortgage payments to increase in the final years. Presumably, in three or four years your income will increase to an extent that will allow you to more easily handle the higher payments.

This plan works best when property values are increasing because the lender will feel more secure in deferring payments if it feels that the security is increasing in value. In this type of repayment plan, payments made at the beginning of the mortgage term may not even cover the full amount of the interest owing. It is necessary, therefore, to capitalize the debt by adding the unpaid interest to the principal, which will of course increase the principal amount of the mortgage. This being the case, the lender wants to make sure that the value of the property stays up so that when the mortgage comes due at the end of its term, if full payment is not made, the lender can recover its money even if the property is sold in a forced sale.

Debts can be rescheduled in many other ways. For example, if you are paid only once every three or six months, it is possible to rewrite the mortgage terms to provide for payments on a semi-annual or quarterly basis rather than have the monthly payments go unpaid and allow late interest to be charged against you.

Any other type of arrangement that may work to your benefit should be explored in depth with the lender.

## b. PROVIDE ADDITIONAL SECURITY

In the days of inflationary increases in property values, lenders were not as concerned with default due to non-payment to the extent they are now. There was always the good possibility that the land could be sold, even in a forced or judicial sale, and make enough money to pay everything that was owed.

When property values drop, however, lenders worry that in a forced sale, they may not recover the full amount of the arrears. Lenders are, therefore, much quicker to start legal action these days than they were in the past, simply to sell before property values drop any further.

To satisfy this concern of the lender, you can offer additional security as part of the mortgage loan. This may not be an alternative for many people, but if you have other properties or assets that can be pledged as security to the mortgagee, you should consider it.

If the lender receives something else that it can use as security in a default, the lender may be prepared to hang in with you just a little bit longer even if you are currently unable to make your payments.

The effect of this is that if the mortgage goes into default, the lender has the right not only to have the first property sold to recover the debt but can also sell the other security that has been pledged.

What assets will a lender accept as security? Naturally this question has to be answered by each lender. However, it is safe to predict that another piece of land, especially in the area where the first land is, would be quite attractive. Other assets such as motor vehicles, vans, campers, and mobile homes can be pledged as security. Such items as your home appliances and other types of personal property, including coin or art collections, photographic equipment, boats, or any other valuable asset you own may be acceptable. Don't forget term deposits, life insurance policies, stocks or bonds or interests in businesses or revenue producing properties.

You may also simply give your personal promissory note. You then are agreeing to become personally liable for the amount owing under the mortgage. If the property is sold and insufficient funds are recovered from the sale, you are going to be personally liable for the shortfall. You can be sued on the promissory note. If a judgment is obtained, any of your assets can be seized to cover the debt. You are potentially placing at risk everything that you own. When particular assets are pledged, only the pledged assets are at risk.

These types of security are known as "collateral security." It can be a useful way of satisfying the lender and keeping the mortgage current. But you may simply be getting in deeper and deeper. Therefore, before you pledge collateral security, consider it carefully.

## c. PAY OFF SOME OF THE PRINCIPAL

If your payments are too high to meet monthly, you can reduce the payments by reducing the principal owing under the mortgage. If the principal is reduced, the interest owing on the principal also has to come down. The difficulty, of course, is coming up with the money to reduce the principal.

One alternative available to many young couples is to utilize liquid assets that their parents have. In some situations it is possible for parents to make a gift to their children on a tax-free basis. Those funds can be used to pay off a portion of the mortgage. The children can then make "gifts" to their parents on an annual or semi-annual basis equivalent to some form of interest rate which might be half or less than half of the rate owing under the mortgage. Because the money is given from adult to adult, there is no tax payable on these transactions. This ultimately means that both parties end up with a better deal, and interest payments under the mortgage are reduced.

Contact an accountant or lawyer to properly review this idea for you.

You might also want to consider using personal term deposits or even RRSP deposits. This is basically a business decision that you will have to make. In all likelihood you will be paying more interest under your mortgage than you will be earning on your term deposits or RRSPs. Because the interest under the mortgage is not tax deductible, you are making your mortgage payments with after tax dollars. In addition, except for the first $1 000, the rest of the income that you receive from interest is taxable.

If you have already accumulated a sizable RRSP you may want to consider transferring it into a self-directed RRSP that controls or contains your own mortgage. Check with an accountant for full details.

Given those factors, it may be cheaper for you to use these funds to pay off your mortgage principal as quickly as possible. For every dollar of principal you pay on your mortgage, you are probably saving yourself at least three or four dollars in interest.

If you can arrange private loans from friends or families at lower interest rates than you would pay on your mortgage, this is also an acceptable alternative. On the other hand, there is no point in borrowing against one asset to pay money owing on another asset. I do not recommend a loan be taken out on a vehicle or other asset to be used to pay on your mortgage unless the loan interest is tax deductible or some other benefit is derived from the loan.

Proper tax planning can set you up so that you can, effectively, use your mortgage payments as a tax deduction. For this, additional assets are required and proper tax planning with an expert is recommended.

You should also remember that prior to making these principal payments on the mortgage, it is necessary to ensure that the mortgage allows "lump sum" payments to be made. Some of the older mortgages do not allow large payments of principal except at the end of the mortgage term. Check with the lender directly or read your mortgage agreement to see if they will consent to a principal payment. In most cases, the lender will probably agree to that payment given the current economic conditions. But it is within the lender's rights to refuse the prepayment if the mortgage does not allow the lump sum payment to be made.

If you are in the midst of renewing your mortgage, it is always a good idea to ensure there is a clause in the mortgage allowing you to make additional payments of principal above your regular monthly payments. In other words, try to get an "open" mortgage.

There is a school of thought that says, rather than reduce the principal, borrowers should "lever" the equity in their home and take out as much cash as possible against the value of the house. The money can be used for investments that will provide a return sufficient to cover the increased mortgage payments plus provide an additional profit. In many provinces, this is a relatively safe investment because if the borrower is unable to make the payments, the worst that can happen is that the property itself will be lost. There will be no personal liability. For example, this is the situation in Alberta and Saskatchewan.

This practice was much more popular two or three years ago than it is today. Because of increasing property values, the lender felt that the security would be good at all times. And the borrower felt that the use of the money for investment purposes would more than cover the payments.

Today, lenders are much more reluctant to make large loans unless the individual can show the ability to keep the payments current without the outside income. In addition, borrowers do not wish to be saddled with large mortgage payments when they are not even sure whether or not their jobs are secure.

## d. GIVE THE PROPERTY TO THE LENDER

One of the consequences of default is its effect on your credit rating and ability to carry on business or borrow.

If you have no other alternatives, you can enter into a "quit claim" agreement with the lender and voluntarily return the property. However, by choosing this alternative, you give up any equity you have in the property.

The quit claim deed is a contract entered into between the mortgagee and mortgagor. It transfers all of the borrower's rights, title, and equity in the property to the lender. The lender does not have to go to court and this saves time and cost.

The advantage of the quit claim to you is that you avoid the frustration and embarrassment of going through a court procedure. Your credit rating is not affected because there is no court action. It is unlikely that the fact of your turning over the property to the mortgagee will be communicated to the credit bureaus or the banks. It may even be possible for you to enter into a separate arrangement with the lender to rent the property if you are particularly attached to it. Many lenders, pending sale of the property, are happy to have tenants occupy the premises to prevent vandalism.

The quit claim agreement has to be agreed to by the lender. In cases of insured CMHC and MICC mortgages, it may be more difficult to obtain the consent of the mortgage company because the lender is guaranteed the repayment of the loan one way or the other.

In addition, a quit claim agreement will not be effective if there are additional mortgages or other encumbrances on the property. For example, it would be impossible to enter into a quit claim agreement with a first mortgagee if there was a second and third mortgage on the title unless the first mortgagee was prepared to accept the property subject to the second and third mortgage.

## e. REFINANCE

The business of lending money is very competitive. Just as it is possible to shop around for a house or anything else you want, it is possible to shop for a mortgage. The criteria that mortgage companies have for making loans vary.

If you want to refinance property when your mortgage is about to fall, or has already fallen, into arrears and some legal action has commenced, you do not have a great deal of bargaining power with other lenders. Lenders are reluctant to lend in a situation where the borrower has defaulted under another loan. Additionally, lenders like to use credit bureaus to obtain credit checks on potential borrowers and most mortgage foreclosure actions find their way into credit bureau files.

It may be best to use the services of a third party to arrange the financing. A mortgage broker, for a fee of about 1% of the principal amount of the mortgage, can arrange a new mortgage for you.

A broker has a number of lending sources and can also present a better and more attractive package to the lender as far as the financing is concerned. Therefore, if the brokerage fee means the difference between finding new financing and not finding new financing, in many cases it is money well spent. Brokers are especially effective in situations where default has occurred or a mortgage has expired.

Shop around for a broker. The rates of mortgage brokers differ quite dramatically as do their services and ability to perform. There are many reputable brokers operating in every province. Normally the brokers are members of a formal group or association. Contacting those organizations might be a good starting point in locating the services of a good broker.

## f. DO NOTHING

We have discussed a number of things you can try if your mortgage is drifting into arrears. One alternative is to do nothing. This is the easiest answer in the short term, although ultimately it will have fairly serious consequences.

For you to decide to do nothing, you would have to have either absolutely no intention of taking any steps to preserve the property or no equity in it. It is simply foolish to take no steps if you have a large equity in the property because it may be rapidly eroded or lost completely. The only time that inaction makes some sort of sense is when you have no equity in the property and there is no prospect of either a sale of the property or any other development that could allow you to bring up the arrears.

If you do nothing, you become in effect a tenant of the property subject to removal once the necessary court proceedings have been concluded. During the period of this tenancy, you will not have to pay "rent" or any other obligations under the mortgage, such as insurance or taxes. In some provinces, depending on the equity in the property, this situation can continue for six months or more.

# 10

## YOUR RIGHTS AFTER
## LEGAL ACTION HAS BEGUN

It is important to realize that no matter how minor the breach or how small the amount of the arrears, the lender has the right to take legal action. As is common throughout our legal system, any party may begin legal action against any other party simply by filing the necessary forms.

This chapter discusses *your* rights, such as your right to stay in the house or sell it, once the action has begun.

### a. HOW LONG WILL THE FORECLOSURE TAKE?

The question of timing is sometimes your most important consideration. If the action is going to be a short one, your best alternative may be to simply abandon the premises. If more time is available, you may want to take some steps to sell the property yourself or find alternative financing in order to pay off the mortgage that is in arrears. An action can go on for years or it can be over in 60 days.

Generally, the greater your equity in the property, the longer the foreclosure action takes; the courts attempt to protect the interests of the borrower to the greatest extent possible. If there is a considerable amount of equity, the courts will normally lengthen the action by increasing the redemption period.

The remedy chosen by the lender will often determine the length of the action. If the power of sale remedy is available, the whole action may be over in about 60 days (if the property sells quickly), whereas if you are entitled to a redemption period, the action could take at least one year.

If you intervene in the court action either personally or with a lawyer, the action will take longer than if you simply ignore it.

If you hire a lawyer to act on your behalf, the action will take longer. The court, knowing that you have at least gone to the trouble and expense of hiring a lawyer, will grant your solicitor more rights than if you simply ignored the proceedings or even appeared on your own behalf.

Your lawyer has to ensure that every action of the lender is being carried out properly. If some technical flaw or defect is found in the procedure, the lender may have to start the process over or delay while it is corrected.

While it is not the lawyer's job simply to delay the action, he or she will ensure that you benefit from all the time that the court can make available to you as part of the normal procedure.

## b. YOUR RIGHT TO LIVE IN YOUR HOUSE

One of the rights of borrowers is exclusive possession of the mortgaged property. This right remains in effect even though legal action has been started. You are innocent until proven guilty. In a mortgage action, you have no legal liability until the court has made a decision about the rights and liabilities of both parties.

As mentioned before, a mortgagee in possession is entitled to take possession of the property except when the borrower actually lives there. It is very unusual for a court to turn out the borrower in a situation involving a residential property. Courts normally are very sympathetic to a borrower in an action that involves his or her residence.

## c. YOUR RIGHT TO SELL YOUR HOUSE

Subject to the power of sale remedy that is available to the lender in some provinces, there is no reason why you cannot sell the premises even after legal action has been started.

You are entitled to list the property with a real estate company or to attempt to sell it on your own. If a sale can be made and the money received before the matter is decided by the court, you can meet your obligations to the lender and end the court action. You will have to pay the court costs.

If the sale involves an assumption of the mortgage, make sure that you are legally entitled to end the action simply by paying up the arrears and the costs. There are circumstances where this may not be possible. Legal advice is recommended.

Must (or should) you disclose to a potential puchaser that some action has been commenced on the mortgage? Sometimes the matter will be taken out of your hands. The lender is entitled to register a special document on the title to your property known as a certificate of lis pendens. The lis pendens is designed to give notice to anybody searching your title that an action has been commenced on the property.

A purchaser who finds out that an action has begun may get cold feet. However, as long as the mortgage is either to be paid off or the arrears to be brought up, there is no risk to the purchaser. The action is a personal action against the homeowner and will not affect the purchaser. Naturally it is important for the purchaser, before completing the sale, to ensure that the action has been discharged or discontinued.

A smart purchaser may want to wait and try to get the property as a result of the court procedure underway. A purchaser could do this either by tendering on the property or waiting until it goes to auction. The risk is that somebody else may come in with a higher bid and the purchaser will lose any chance of buying the property. However, the purchaser may be prepared to take that risk in return for a chance to get the property at a lower price.

Therefore, it is in your best interests to say that there is an action going on and to work with the purchaser in trying to overcome the problems involved. This will increase your credibility while negotiating on the sale. Because buying and selling real estate is such an emotional business, this may play an important part in the ultimate decision by the purchaser.

## d. DO YOU HAVE TO SHOW YOUR HOUSE?

Subject to the mortgagee's remedies already discussed, you are not obliged to show anyone the property during the time of the court action.

You may, of course, co-operate with the lender and allow people in to view the house. This may be beneficial to you in the long run because it might ultimately mean a higher price for the property and perhaps some money left over for you after the smoke has cleared and all other costs have been paid.

An appraiser is hired by the lender to provide the court with a fair market value of the property. The court uses this information to decide such things as the length of the redemption period or the amount of equity in the property.

You do not have to allow the appraiser inside your home in which case he or she will simply do a "drive-by" appraisal. This is not a full appraisal and any of the special or valuable aspects of your house may be ignored. Nevertheless, the courts will usually accept the appraisal, no matter how sketchy it is.

The lender wants as low an appraisal as possible in order to reduce the equity that you have. Although appraisers are not instructed to provide low appraisals, the values obtained in mortgage actions are often quite low. One way to counteract this is to allow the appraiser access to your house and to point out all of the improvements that you have made. The other alternative is to obtain your own appraisal. You can use your own appraisal to offset claims made by the lender that you have little or no equity in your property.

## e. DO YOU HAVE TO MAKE PAYMENTS?

Although interest continues to accrue while court action is ongoing and the legal costs can mount up, there is no advantage to you in making payments while the action continues.

Once the action has begun, it is only in your best interests to make a payment if it will do some good. For example, there are circumstances where you can apply to the court asking for a longer redemption period in exchange for payment of some money due. Depending on the equity position and the discretion of the court, the court can use this payment as grounds for extending the redemption period.

Sometimes, a partial payment can be used to convince the lender to suspend the action for a period of time. This requires some negotiation on your part.

## f. WHAT HAPPENS IF A BUYER ASSUMES YOUR MORTGAGE?

The basic rule is that the current registered owner of the property is primarily liable under the mortgage. This can be either the original borrower or someone who has assumed that mortgage.

There are basically two ways to assume a mortgage of residential property. One is to obtain the consent of the lender when the property is being sold. The other is to take the property over and automatically assume the mortgage without obtaining the consent of the lender.

Depending on the province and the circumstances involved in the mortgage, a new home buyer taking over an existing mortgage will have to find out if the lender's consent is required.

In Alberta and Saskatchewan, for example, the current law seems to suggest that any mortgage, unless it is a collateral mortgage, is assumable. This is the case despite the fact that the mortgage normally contains an acceleration clause that would allow the lender to demand the balance of the mortgage upon sale. In other provinces, it is best to check with a lawyer to find out if that mortgage can be taken over. It may be that all that is required is to be approved by the lender. Traditionally, the qualification requirements for an assumption are much less stringent than the requirements for a new mortgage application.

A buyer who assumes your mortgage becomes responsible for the mortgage payments that you did not make, although most people would not assume a mortgage that is in default.

Because of the unique nature of the mortgage agreement, and the fact that laws dealing with land and property rights are somewhat different than ordinary contractual laws, once your mortgage is assumed by someone else, any liability you may have had under the mortgage may be discharged.

If you are named in an action on property where you no longer reside, I suggest you obtain immediate legal advice to ensure that you have no liability to the lender.

# 11

## YOUR LEGAL DEFENCE

This very technical area involves statutes and rules of practice. The laws in each province are surprisingly different insofar as the actual foreclosure, judicial sale or other type of action is concerned. However, the basic remedies available to a borrower are quite similar in each province.

You can either actively defend the lender's action or do nothing. By defending the action you may be able to buy the extra time you need to sell, refinance or simply bail out.

However, if you have no equity in your property there may not be a great deal to gain in becoming actively involved in the mortgage action. You must ask yourself whether it would be worth your while to try to keep the property for yourself. In effect, any money that you already put into the property in down payments, monthly mortgage payments or improvements will be lost since the lender has first claim to the proceeds of a sale. Therefore, unless there is money left over for you after the mortgage is paid, there is no reason to try to redeem the mortgage or sell the property. The property may become a liability to you just as it is a liability to the mortgagee.

If there *is* some equity in the property, there may be something worth fighting for. The fact that you are in arrears may only be temporary based on some unusual economic factor such as a temporary work lay-off. If this is the case, you may be able to get back on your feet and either save the money or borrow enough money to redeem the mortgage if you have some extra time.

You must be realistic when facing a mortgage action on your home. If the value of your property will continue to drop, further reducing your equity, or if the prospects of a sale are bleak because of a bad real estate market, it may be advantageous to simply cut your losses as soon as possible.

Alternatively, if property values are rising, your equity is increasing, and the prospects of a sale are good, you may have a chance to save your house. Many people in the late seventies were able to avoid the loss of their homes for this reason. Therefore, a careful assessment of the outside market is important.

## a. WHAT LEGAL DEFENCES ARE AVAILABLE?

You may have grounds to defend the action if any of the following apply to your situation.

(a) You dispute the amount of principal the lender is claiming or has calculated as owing on the mortgage

(b) You dispute the calculation of the interest the lender is claiming from you or the method of calculating interest

(c) You deny some or all of the claims for non-payment made by the lender, or your records do not correspond with the apparent information that the lender has

(d) You dispute the claim of non-payment of taxes, insurance or some other amount not associated with the normal mortgage payments, or you deny responsibility for these items

(e) You dispute the facts on which a non-monetary claim is based, e.g., that you have not damaged the premises. It will normally require a judicial decision to determine the rights of the parties.

(f) There are defects in the preparation or registration of the mortgage document

If you dispute either the original mortgage amount, the interest rate, the term or any other major clause in the mortgage agreement, or if the terms of the mortgage do not correspond with either the original commitment letter you received or the representations made to you by the lender, you may have a defence based on the legal doctrines of *non est factum* and negligent misrepresentation.

## b. SHOULD YOU HIRE A LAWYER?

Because of the highly technical nature of the mortgage action, both the lender and borrower must comply with all legal requirements. The first decision you must make is whether or not to hire a lawyer.

There is no point in spending money on a lawyer unless you have a particular goal in mind.

If you have any of the defences discussed previously, I strongly recommend that you obtain legal counsel — you will be involved in a long civil litigation procedure. But only a small percentage of mortgage actions involve these issues.

The most common reason that borrowers become actively involved in the mortgage action is to buy time to sell the premises, to save money to redeem the premises, or to live there as long as possible, at basically no cost until they are forced to move. In these cases there is no dispute with the fact that there has been a default.

A lawyer is able to make sure that the lender's lawyer follows all the correct procedures. In order for a lender to "win" a mortgage action, it must follow to the letter all the legal requirements of your province. Without someone trained in the technicalities overseeing the process, the lender may take shortcuts. A lawyer will ensure that your rights are protected; this process may result in prolonging the action and giving you additional time.

However, in making a decision about hiring a lawyer under those circumstances, you should consider whether you can afford to pay a lawyer.

No lawyer is going to work for a borrower who is in default without either a very large retainer or some other form of security. It may be that you simply do not have the money for a lawyer.

Your only alternative then is to seek the assistance of the legal aid program in your province. However, legal aid will probably not pay a lawyer's fees simply to delay a mortgage action. There will have to be some other valid defence.

Unfortunately, legal aid is a catch-22 situation. In many jurisdictions, if you have equity in your house, you will not qualify for legal aid. However, if you do not have equity in your house, there may be nothing worth preserving and legal aid may turn you down for that reason.

In addition, you must consider whether the money you would pay to a lawyer would be better spent in other ways. You could hire a mortgage broker to arrange new financing for you to pay off the mortgage that is in arrears. You could use the money to market the property with advertisements and other marketing methods that could help sell the property and get you out from under. Finally, you could pay it to the lender directly. This would only be effective if the lender were prepared to give you something in return such as an additional period of time in the house. In other words, if you owe $100 000, a payment of $1 000 will probably not have a great effect in slowing down the action.

# 12

## OTHER EFFECTS
## OF A MORTGAGE ACTION

A mortgage action will affect not only the property involved, but may have serious ramifications on other aspects of your life. This chapter discusses the effects while an action is ongoing and after an action has been concluded whether or not you have been able to redeem the mortgage.

## a. THE EFFECT ON YOUR CREDIT RATING

Any action involving a mortgage involves litigation. Even those remedies that a lender has that do not automatically involve going to court are always subject to court scrutiny. When an action is started on your mortgage, you are being sued.

Because this action, like all litigation actions, involves filing court documents, information about it is part of the public record. This means that any person can find out that there is a lawsuit against you and the details of that lawsuit, but usually the general public is not interested. The information is normally not circulated to the media, employers, creditors or any other member of the public.

However, credit reporting agencies that are in the business of providing credit reports and information to lenders, employers or businesses do obtain this information. It can find its way into your credit file. Even though there is no liability until the court decides the rights of the parties, the fact that litigation was begun against you is often reported to the credit reporting agencies.

In addition, there are companies that provide a weekly run-down of "who is suing who" to a list of subscribers. The information is obtained directly from the court file and is used by the subscribers for any number of reasons.

This information, if it does find its way to a credit reporting agency, can be harmful to your credit rating even if the action is later terminated because you redeem or sell the property. The information can affect future attempts you make at borrowing or obtaining new mortgage financing. Most lenders, conservative in nature, become even more conservative in tight economic times. Even the slightest hint that you may not make good on a mortgage loan might be enough to convince someone not to lend to you. This may apply even when you try to get a credit card.

If an action against you is discontinued because you either redeemed or paid off the mortgage, obtain confirmation in writing from the lender that the action has been concluded. You should also get a copy of the discontinuance documents from the lender or the lender's lawyer. You are entitled to these documents. You can either keep them until you apply for future financing or send them to the credit reporting agencies in your area to ensure that their file is updated.

Under the laws in Canada, you are entitled to examine the files maintained by credit bureaus and to report any discrepancies in those files. It is wise to check your file from time to time and make sure that the information in it is accurate.

The credit reporting agencies also obtain information about final judgments or other court orders that are granted.

If a judgment has been made against you, it is more damaging on your credit rating and may definitely affect your future ability to borrow on credit.

As soon as you are able to satisfy the court order or judgment, you should obtain proof that you have properly dealt with the obligations imposed by the court on you. With this information, you can ensure that the credit reporting agencies' files are accurate and current. In addition, you can use these papers to satisfy potential lenders that you are indeed trustworthy and a good credit risk.

## b. THE EFFECT ON FUTURE MORTGAGE APPLICATIONS

There is no standard answer about whether a lender will automatically refuse to grant you a mortgage if you have defaulted on a previous one. The attitudes of lenders differ depending upon the place and the type of property.

The new lender will consider the amount of equity you will be putting into the new property, your financial position at the time, and your ability to keep up with the payments.

If you put a substantial amount down on a property and prove that you can afford the monthly mortgage payments, it is quite likely that the new lender would approve a mortgage loan.

However, if it looks like there could be a problem with your application because something in it is unacceptable, you can use the services of a mortgage broker. As discussed earlier, a mortgage broker often has a greater number of sources for loans and can be more successful in obtaining one for you.

## c. THE EFFECT OF A BANKRUPTCY ON YOUR MORTGAGE

The default under your mortgage may be just part of a larger problem. You may be unable to make other payments and may be heavily indebted to many other creditors in addition to the mortgagee. Should you declare bankruptcy?

Each situation is different, but the simple fact that a mortgage has fallen into arrears or that an action has been started against you should not automatically make you consider bankruptcy. This is especially true if you have a large equity in the property or if your financial problems are temporary. Bankruptcy is an ultimate remedy and will have far-reaching effects on every aspect of your life. If the problem on your mortgage is an isolated one and all of your other finances are in good order, bankruptcy should not be considered.

It is also important to consider the mortgaged property. If it is your personal residence, there is probably more reason to avoid bankruptcy than if the default affects revenue property. The courts will often try to assist you when it is your personal residence but, in many provinces, you are not personally liable for the mortgage debt, although you can ultimately lose the property and your equity in it.

As well, in many provinces, some of the proceeds from the sale of your mortgaged home are exempt from creditors. For example, in Alberta, the first $40 000 of proceeds per owner is exempt from bankruptcy or any other proceedings. This means that a husband and wife who are co-owners are entitled to the first $80 000 of sale proceeds after the mortgages have been cleared. This $80 000 goes to them in priority to all other unsecured creditors.

If the action on the mortgage is part of a general business failure, then, of course, bankruptcy must be considered. In bankruptcy, it will be up to the trustee to decide whether or not you will be able to remain in your house. The trustee realizes that you need a place to live and that you are entitled to maintain a reasonable standard of living, even while in bankruptcy.

The decision will probably be based on the amount of money needed to maintain the mortgage. It is well within the trustee's rights to require you to rent cheaper premises during the period of bankruptcy, meaning your house will have to be sold.

The trustee will be advised by the creditor's representatives who may or may not feel that you should be entitled to live in the house while going through the bankruptcy process. Naturally, if you are in arrears under the mortgage, the lender may have something to say about the situation. A lender is entitled to begin and continue an action on the mortgage even if you declare bankruptcy. In that case, the action pursued by the lender may determine how long you can live in your house. From a practical point of view, if you are in bankruptcy, the lender will probably be able to hurry the action through much more quickly.

How will bankruptcy affect your equity in your home? The first thing to note is that the lender, under bankruptcy law, is a secured creditor. Under Canadian law, a secured creditor is not affected by bankruptcy to any great extent. In the case of your home, the land provides security to the lender. This means that upon bankruptcy, the lender has a right to the proceeds from the sale of the property before all your other creditors get paid anything.

In a bankruptcy, a trustee is appointed to handle the collection and sale of all your assets. If your mortgaged property is sold, any money left over after the lender has been paid will be used to pay your other creditors. However, the lender gets first crack at the money that comes from the property, and, as mentioned, some provinces allow you to keep a specified amount from the proceeds before paying your other creditors.

If the sale of the property does not cover the full amount of the debt owing to the lender, as far as the shortfall is concerned, the mortgagee is considered as an unsecured creditor in a bankruptcy.

For example, assume that you have a mortgage for $50 000 on your property. You declare bankruptcy and the property is sold on a forced sale basis for $40 000. Assume that there are 10 other unsecured creditors who are owed a total of $100 000. They do not have a mortgage or other security. The lender is entitled to all of the $40 000 out of the proceeds of the sale of the mortgaged property. The other $10 000 owed to the lender is added to the amount owed to the other 10 creditors. Therefore, the total amount of your unsecured debt is $110 000. If your other assets are sold for $55 000, all the unsecured creditors, including your lender, will have to divide up this amount. They will each receive about half what they are owed. So the lender would ultimately endure a net loss of $5 000.

## d. THE EFFECT ON YOUR OTHER ASSETS

Initially, only the property that forms part of the mortgage security is at risk. If it is a blanket mortgage, i.e., a mortgage that covers more than one property, then all of the properties are at risk.

Your other assets will be affected only if the lender sues you under your personal covenant. If the lender has the right to get a personal judgment against you for an amount still owing after the mortgaged property is sold, then your other assets are at risk. Once a judgment has been granted against you, certain of your assets can be seized and sold to pay off the debt.

These rights are given to a judgment creditor by law to allow the creditor the opportunity to be repaid. The creditor is entitled to question a debtor under oath in order to find out what assets the debtor has.

Not all assets are available to creditors. Each province "exempts" certain assets owned by debtors and makes it illegal to remove or seize them. Because the exempt assets vary from province to province, you should check with either a lawyer or the sheriff's office in your area to see if a particular asset is exempt.

Legal assistance may be necessary to ensure that your rights are properly dealt with in this situation.

## e. THE EFFECT ON
## SECOND OR THIRD MORTGAGES

It is quite common to have more than one mortgage on a property. The priority to the security in the land is based on the date of registration of the mortgage. Therefore, the first mortgage registered on the property has prior rights to all other mortgages.

A clause in the second or third mortgage can turn a default under the first mortgage into a default under the second or third mortgage. These clauses have been held legally valid. The effect is to give the second or third mortgagee the right to begin an action under its own mortgage if a default has occurred on another mortgage.

Even if the first lender does not start an action in a default of its mortgage, the second or third lender may begin the action even if the second or third mortgage itself is not in default.

What this means, of course, is that an action by a lender may trigger a second action by the subsequent mortgagee. However, the situation does not work in reverse. If there is a default under a second mortgage and the first mortgage remains in good standing, the first mortgagee is unable to begin an action.

An action by a lender on one property will not affect the rights of a lender who holds a mortgage on another of your properties unless the two properties contain the same blanket mortgage.

If your second mortgagee is becoming very nervous because an action has been started by the first mortgagee, keep making the second mortgage payments on time and keep good lines of communication open.

What should you do if you have two mortgages on your property and you can only afford to pay on one of them?

This is a common problem, and it has no simple solution. You have many alternatives open to you, but they all will leave you in default of either one or both of your mortgages. Sometimes part payments to each will take the immediate heat off and forestall action by either of them. However, if it comes to a choice between mortgages, pay the second before the first.

The interest rate on the second will be higher and therefore non-payment will eat your equity away faster than non-payment on the first mortgage. Second, because there is more equity in the property under the first mortgage than the second mortgage, an action by the first mortgagee will normally take much longer to conclude.

## f. THE EFFECT ON YOUR SPOUSE

If your spouse is one of the owners of the property, the mortgage action will name your spouse as a defendent or party to the action simply because he or she signed the mortgage contract. Once a breach occurs, the lender is entitled to name all of the borrowers as party to the action.

Occasionally, the lender may not name a spouse as part of the action; this is for public relations purposes or because the lender thinks that the spouse has no personal assets. In the vast majority of cases, however, the lender names all of the parties to the mortgage agreement as defendents or respondents in the action.

If the parties own the property as an undivided interest rather than as joint tenants or tenants in common, then it is possible to place the mortgage over the undivided interest of one party and not the other.

For example, assume that Mr. and Mrs. Equity have acquired a home. Because the down payment came equally from Mr. Equity's family and Mrs. Equity's family, they decided that when one of them died, the title to the property should go back to their respective parents. Accordingly, they each hold an undivided 50% interest in the property. Because Mrs. Equity's parents gave her enough money to pay half the cost of the house, it was only necessary for Mr. Equity to obtain a mortgage to cover the balance of his half of the investment. Mr. Equity obtained a mortgage that was registered only against his undivided 50% interest in the land. In an action against Mr. Equity, the lender can only go against his undivided half of the property. Mrs. Equity would not be named as a party to that action. She would not be affected by the action except to the extent of her dower rights, which are discussed below.

In summary then, depending on the interest held, if the spouses own the property jointly, then an action against one spouse will normally include the other spouse. Because the spouses hold the interest as joint tenants, or tenants in common, they are both jointly and severally liable on the mortgage. The interest of both parties in the land is at risk. In addition, the lender can proceed against either or both parties for the full debt that remains outstanding.

If the spouse is not one of the owners of the property, the situation is somewhat different. There are differences within this category depending on whether or not the property is a "homestead."

A homestead is your personal residence (house, quarter section of land, mobile home, boat, condominium or townhouse). In many provinces, spouses who are not owners of property have "dower rights," which must be taken into consideration in a mortgage action.

Basically, dower rights give a spouse the right to live on the property for life or the right to a certain interest in the property even if the spouse did not put any money into the property or is not a named owner. Dower rights take effect only on the death of the registered owner or the sale of the property.

Dower rights are provided for spouses in Alberta, British Columbia, and Saskatchewan. In Manitoba, the widow's common law right to dower has been abolished and replaced by a new statutory right of possession for a spouse residing in the matrimonial home. In Ontario, no spouse may dispose of, or place a mortgage on, a matrimonial home unless the other spouse joins in or consents to the transaction.

When a mortgage is taken out on matrimonial or homestead property that is not registered in the name of both spouses, the lender requires the unnamed spouse to consent to the mortgage. A special form is attached to each mortgage. It is the "dower consent," and the spouse normally is asked to sign it apart from the other spouse and with the assistance of separate legal counsel. This is to ensure that the unnamed spouse is made fully aware of the dower rights that are relinquished once the consent is signed.

When a spouse has signed a dower consent on the mortgage agreement, the lender is free to take whatever legal action against the property that may be necessary without having to worry about dower rights. In other words, the lender can proceed against the property and will have priority over the dower rights of the spouse.

If the property is not a homestead property and the title is not in your spouse's name, your spouse will not be named in the action or have any of his or her assets at risk.

Of course, if your spouse signed any security, such as a promissory note or personal guarantee to a collateral mortgage, then he or she is liable.

## g. THE EFFECT OF A DIVORCE

In a divorce, matrimonial property laws provide for an equitable distribution of property between the two parties. If an action on the mortgage begins prior to any divorce action, the status of the parties will not be affected by matrimonial property legislation. If the property is lost in a foreclosure or judicial sale, it simply ceases to be part of the matrimonial property and will not have to be dealt with if there is a divorce later.

The only time when matrimonial property rights may complicate a situation is when a divorce/matrimonial property action occurs at the same time as an action on the mortgage. This is not altogether unusual because financial setback and failure is one of the major causes of divorce in Canada.

If these two problems occur at the same time, especially if there is equity in the matrimonial property, steps will have to be taken to protect the rights of the spouses. Matrimonial property legislation in the various provinces usually allows a postponement or delay of the action on the mortgage until the situation between the spouses is clarified.

The same situation applies when spouses are co-owners of property other than their matrimonial residence. Investment property is part of the matrimonial property assets, so any action by the lender is limited in the same way as for the matrimonial residence.

These situations can become very complicated. Legal advice is required for both spouses so that each party's rights are fully protected.

## h. THE EFFECT ON PERSONAL LIABILITY

If the lender is successful in an action, it will have judgment against you. Unlike other types of litigation, however, the judgment or court order will primarily affect the land that forms part of the mortgage security. After all, the lender made the loan to you primarily because you put some land up as security. Lenders must proceed initially against the land. But if the land is sold and returns less than the amount required to clear the full debt, the lender may be able to obtain a personal judgment against you for this shortfall.

As discussed earlier, laws in Alberta and Saskatchewan relieve borrowers from any personal liability on conventional mortgages. Therefore, in almost all situations involving personal residences and mortgage action for default, the remedy of the lender is limited to the land only. The lender in those provinces is entitled to either sell the land and use the proceeds to reduce or pay off the loan or to take title to the property.

In Manitoba, British Columbia, and Ontario, you do have some potential liability under the personal covenant provision in the mortgage. Depending on the type of remedy pursued by the lender, you may be personally liable.

If the lender sells the property instead of taking title to it, and a shortfall results, personal liability may result. However, once title goes into the name of the lender under some form of foreclosure order, the lender may lose its rights to sue you personally. This varies from province to province (see chapter 8).

If you have a collateral mortgage and personal action is begun against you, I recommend that you seek legal advice in order to determine your liability. Other assets besides the mortgage property may be at risk.

Note that the personal covenant on the mortgage remains in force, even though you may have sold the property, unless the lender has agreed to release you from any personal liability. The situation may become complicated. Borrower A sells property to B, who assumes the mortgage. Borrower B then sells the property to C, who assumes the mortgage. If the property falls into arrears while C has the mortgage, what is the liability of parties A and B? In Ontario, party B is relieved of obligation although parties A and C are not. In other provinces, liability potentially rests with parties A, B, and C, although the courts would in all likelihood relieve parties A and B from liability.

## i. INCOME TAX CONSIDERATIONS

Unfortunately, the bad news of a foreclosure action may also mean some bad news from an income tax point of view. Certain sections of the Income Tax Act may be applicable if your house ends up with your lender as a consequence of your default. The effect of these sections would be to assess you with a form of capital gain. In most cases, the tax consequences are minimal, but you should alert your accountant of the foreclosure situation prior to the preparation and filing of your personal income tax return.

## j. THE COSTS OF A MORTGAGE ACTION

One of the clauses in the mortgage that you signed in all likelihood requires you to be responsible for all costs associated with an action by the lender. You are responsible for all of the costs involved in a mortgage action from the date of the demand letter until the date that the property is finally either redeemed, sold or foreclosed upon.

What are these costs?

Because of the technical nature of a mortgage action, the vast majority of lenders hire lawyers to take charge of the action. They do this in order to ensure that it is done properly and that all the rules are followed. They also want to eliminate technical errors in the procedure to avoid delays.

Each province has a tariff of costs for this type of action. These costs are known as the "taxable costs" that the courts allow the lawyer to charge. Although it is impossible to say how much those taxable costs will be, it is obvious that they will increase the longer the action continues.

Therefore, if you pay the arrears as soon as you receive the demand letter, you will only be responsible for payment of costs between $50 and $75. If the foreclosure action takes a year to a year and one-half, the costs could very well go up around $1 000 to $2 500.

In addition to the taxable costs, some provinces also allow what are known as "solicitor-client costs" to be charged to the borrower. Taxable costs do not normally cover the full amount of the time spent by the lender's lawyer on each particular action. The solicitor-client cost is what the lawyer charges the lender for legal services. These solicitor-client costs are usually higher than taxable costs; they can run into thousands of dollars.

One of the advantages of having a lawyer act on your behalf in a mortgage action is that he or she will monitor these costs as they continue to mount up. You have the right to contest the costs in order to ensure that they are within the established tariff or are reasonable in the circumstances. The process of reviewing these costs is known as "taxation" and can be effective in keeping the costs down as much as possible.

You will also, of course, be responsible for your own lawyer's costs.

## k. CONCLUSION

As we have seen, there are many varieties to the basic mortgage agreement. The variations introduced to mortgages over the years are more a response to the marketplace than an attempt to trap the unwary borrower. When you are in the market for a mortgage, remember that although various terms in the mortgage can be altered to reflect your situation, the remedies available are pretty well the same in every case if you run into trouble.

Now that you have read about the rights, remedies, liabilities, responsibilities and obligations of both the borrower and lender, you should be more confident dealing in the field of mortgages. Although a mortgage can be complex and full of technical rules and regulations, many of the concepts are quite simple to understand. Keep this in mind whenever you deal with any aspect of a mortgage.

# CANADIAN
# ORDER FORM
# SELF-COUNSEL SERIES

## PROVINCIAL TITLES

**Divorce Guide**
- ❑ B.C. 9.95 ❑ Alberta 9.95 ❑ Saskatchewan 12.95
- ❑ Manitoba 11.95 ❑ Ontario 12.95

**Employer/Employee Rights**
- ❑ B.C. 7.95 ❑ Alberta 6.95 ❑ Ontario 6.95

**Incorporation Guide**
- ❑ B.C. 14.95 ❑ Alberta 14.95 ❑ Manitoba/Saskatchewan 12.95 ❑ Ontario 14.95

**Landlord/Tenant Rights**
- ❑ B.C. 7.95 ❑ Alberta 6.95 ❑ Ontario 7.95

**Marriage & Family Law**
- ❑ B.C. 7.95 ❑ Alberta 8.95 ❑ Ontario 7.95

**Probate Guide**
- ❑ B.C. 12.95 ❑ Alberta 10.95 ❑ Ontario 11.95

**Real Estate Guide**
- ❑ B.C. 8.95 ❑ Alberta 7.95 ❑ Ontario 8.50

**Small Claims Court Guide**
- ❑ B.C. 7.95 ❑ Alberta 7.50 ❑ Ontario 7.50

**Wills**
- ❑ B.C. 6.50 ❑ Alberta 6.50 ❑ Ontario 5.95
- ❑ Wills/Probate Procedure for Manitoba/Saskatchewan 5.95

## PACKAGED FORMS

**Divorce Forms**
- ❑ B.C 11.95 ❑ Alberta 10.95 ❑ Saskatchewan 12.95
- ❑ Manitoba 10.95 ❑ Ontario 14.95

**Incorporation**
- ❑ B.C 14.95 ❑ Alberta 14.95 ❑ Saskatchewan 14.95
- ❑ Manitoba 14.95 ❑ Ontario 14.95 ❑ Federal 7.95
- ❑ Minute Books 17.95
- ❑ Power of Attorney Kit 9.95

**Probate**
- ❑ B.C. Administration 14.95 ❑ B.C. Probate 14.95
- ❑ Alberta 14.95 ❑ Ontario 15.50
- ❑ Rental Form Kit (B.C., Alberta, Saskatchewan, Ontario) 4.95
- ❑ Have You Made Your Will? 5.95
- ❑ If You Love Me Put It In Writing — Contract Kit 14.95
- ❑ If You Leave Me Put It In Writing — B.C. Separation Agreement Kit 14.95

**Interim Agreement**
- ❑ B.C. 2.50 ❑ Alberta 2.50 ❑ Ontario 2.50

*Note: All prices subject to change without notice.*
Books are available in book and department stores, or use the order form below. Please enclose cheque or money order (plus sales tax where applicable) or give us your MasterCard or Visa number (please include validation and expiry dates).

-✂-------------------------------------------------------------------------

(PLEASE PRINT)
Name _____
Address _____
City _____ Province _____
Postal Code _____
❑ Visa/❑ MasterCard Number_____
Validation Date_____ Expiry Date _____
If order is under $20.00, add $1.00 for postage and handling.
Please send orders to:
**SELF-COUNSEL PRESS**
**1481 Charlotte Road**
**North Vancouver, British Columbia    V7J 1H1**

❑ Check here for free catalogue.